ONE HUNDRED NAMES OF GOD

TORKOM SARAYDARIAN

T.S.G. PUBLISHING FOUNDATION

One Hundred Names of God

© 1995 The Creative Trust

All Rights Reserved: No part of this publication may be reproduced, stored in a retrieval system, or transmitted in any form, by any means, electronic, mechanical, photocopying, recording or otherwise, without permission in writing from the copyright owner or his representatives. Permission to quote freely given. Contact publisher for details.

ISBN: 0-929874-49-8

Library of Congress Catalog Card Number 94-60983

Printed in the United States of America

Cover Design: Tim Fisher
              Phoenix, Arizona

Printed by: *Data Reproductions*
              Rochester Hills, MI 48307

Published by: **T.S.G. Publishing Foundation, Inc.**
              P.O. Box 7068
              Cave Creek, AZ 85331-7068
              United States of America

Note: Meditations and visualizations are given as guidelines. They should be used with discretion and after receiving professional advice.

This is my song,
Sung for thee, my Lord.
Listen only to my
Voice of Love
and ignore my words.

—Torkom Saraydarian

Printed in memory of
Valarshak and Flora Galoostian
with gratitude
Torkom Saraydarian

This book is a transcription of a series of lectures
given by the author in Sedona, Arizona.

Contents

A Few Words		7
Commentary		9
1.	The Compassionate One	15
2.	The All Merciful One	17
3.	The King	19
4.	The Holy One	20
5.	The Peace	21
6.	The Faithful	23
7.	The Guardian	24
8.	The Mighty One	26
9.	The Compeller	28
10.	The Dignified	29
11.	The Creator	30
12.	The Constructor	31
13.	The Fashioner	32
14.	The Motionless One	33
15.	The Conqueror	34
16.	The Best Bestower	35
17.	The Sustainer	36
18.	The Opener	37
19.	The Knower	38
	Q&A	39
	Commentary	43
20.	One Who Expands	46
21.	The Abaser — The Humiliator	48
22.	The Exalter	50
23.	The Strengthener	52
24.	The Dishonorer	53
25.	All-Knowing	56
26.	All-Seeing One	57
27.	The Judge	59
28.	Righteousness	61
29.	The Beauty	62
30.	The Aware One	63
31.	The Patient One	65
32.	The Magnificent	67
33.	The Forgiver	68
34.	Gratitude	70
35.	The Sublime	71
36.	Akbar — The Great	72
37.	The Preserver	73
38.	The Feeder	74
39.	The Redeemer	75
	Q&A	76
	Commentary	81
40.	The Calculator	84
41.	The Majestic	85
42.	The Generous One	87
43.	The Watchful One	90
44.	The Responsive One	93
45.	All-Embracing One	95
46.	The Wise One	97
47.	The Loving One	99
48.	The Gracious One	101
49.	The Resurrecting One	103
50.	The Witness	105
51.	The Truth	107

	Q&A	112
	Commentary	115
53.	The Strong One	120
54.	The Firm One	122
55.	The Protecting Friend	125
56.	The Praiseworthy One	128
57.	The Accountant	131
58.	The Originator	133
59.	The Provider	135
60.	The Quickener	137
61.	The Destroyer	139
	Commentary	141
62.	The Ever-Living	145
63.	The Self-Existing One	147
64.	The Noble One	150
65.	The Glorious One	152
66.	The Unique One	155
67.	The One	157
68.	The Absolute	159
69.	The Able One	161
70.	The Dominant One	165
71.	The Expediter	167
72.	The Postponer	168
73.	The First One	169
	Commentary	171
74.	The Last One	181
75.	The Manifested One	184
	Q&A	189
	Commentary	193
76.	The Internal One	202
77.	The Governor	207
78.	The Most Exhalted One	211
79.	The Devoted One	213
80.	Acceptor of Repentance	216
81.	The Avenger	219
82.	The Tolerant One	221
83.	The Consoling One	222
84.	The Power	224
85.	The Lord of Majesty	225
86.	The Balancing One	226
87.	The Collector	227
88.	The Independent One	228
89.	Bestower of Wealth	229
90.	The Restrainer	230
91.	The Distresser	231
	Q&A	232
92.	Profiter	235
93.	Light	236
94.	The Guide	237
95.	Incomparable	238
96.	Everlasting	239
97.	Inheritor	240
98.	The Path	241
99.	Forbearer	242
100.	Allah — God	244
	Commentary	245
	Index	249

A Few Words

One of my greatest pleasures has been to research the names of God. In these names I saw the people's responses to the Infinite, the degree of their communication with Him, and the depth of their aspiration. Without exaggeration I found more than five thousand names in many religions, traditions, stories, and fairy tales, and I never found any tradition that did not talk about God or about a similar concept.

I knew from the beginning that to know God directly was not possible for me. There were two ways for me to approach Him: One was to meditate on all His revelations — all living forms such as trees, stars, rivers, men, oceans, etc. — because I thought that all manifestation is His revelation. The second was to meditate upon names given Him by all people everywhere.

Once when I was studying Sufism I read about "the hundred names of God." They impressed me so much that I studied them for a long time until I discovered that these hundred names could synthesize all names given in the Vedas about gods or devas, all names given by the Chaldeans, Assyrians, Armenians, Hebrews, American Indians, Aztecs, Mayans, and so on.

For example one of God's names is *AUM*.[1] Another is Fohat and His Seven Brothers, one of Them being a great God of Fire — Agni. Helios, Tao, Tat (That), Vahagn, Anahit, Mazda, Ain Sof, Space, Energy, Consciousness, and Reality are other names.

Future students of wisdom will study all names of God as fragments of a picture puzzle, and eventually they will have an idea of the true characteristics of God.

Modern man has forgotten the inspiring, uplifting, transforming names of God. Instead he has created the golden calf — sex, money, power, bombs.

It is time that the Gods of all countries be united.

In meditating upon these hundred names of God, we may build in our psyche an inner telescope to look beyond the darkness of our spiritual ignorance and discover the glory shining in Infinity.

> *In the name of God, Most Gracious, Most Merciful.*
>
> — Koran

---

1. For more information, see Ch. 24 in *Cosmos in Man*.

In this age we must expand our understanding of the word *God*. In primitive times people thought that every river had a god, every mountain had a god, every star had a god, the earth had its god, the solar system had its god, so they thought that God was many gods.

Slowly this idea is changing. We are finding out that there is only one God. But what God is we do not know. If we sit down and sincerely write about our understanding of the word God, we will find that we do not know anything.

We take it for granted that we know God, what He is, and we talk with God. For example, a very advanced Saint used to shake the branches of trees and say, "Hi, God. How are You?" What he understood by the term, *God*, who knows?

When Saint Augustine spoke about God he said, "God is taste. When I say *God*, my lips become sugary." God is taste. Another Saint said, "God is perfume, fragrance." Another one said, "God is joy; God is touch; God is melody, symphony." I think all of them are right, but there is no complete idea yet of what God is.

How can the idea of God slowly find real roots within our soul?

First of all through science — when we know what the creation is and what the laws are, we can raise ourselves from the primitive ideas and start thinking, "God is not what I am thinking He is. God is something greater and greater and greater. All of my assumptions and ideas are nothing else but a measure of my understanding — of my beingness."

I understood this very well when I was visiting a home. Two boys were playing with wooden blocks. I asked, "What are you doing?" They replied, "We are building the Universe." Then one of them kicked the building, destroying it, and started laughing. Then they started to build it again. The Universe for them was that construction of blocks.

Humanity builds like that with "blocks." "God is this; God is that; God spoke to me." Really? Did God really speak to you? Then why does it say in the Bible that when we see Him, we will be like Him? Saint Paul, speaking about God, "escaped" very sneakily; he did not define God. He said, "In the future when we see Him, we will be like Him." There is no definition.

Now the first way to find an idea of God is to study the world. Study the flowers, the rivers, the energies, the forces, the cycles in the Universe. Look at the stars and have a little idea of what the Creator is.

The second means is to read religions and philosophies. Get an idea of God without forgetting one thing — *all that is given is passed through a human mind, and the human mind is a "broken glass" reflecting the Sun.* How can you say that the reflection is God? There is no human being who can comprehend, encompass the idea of God in his mind and say, "This is it. God is this."

The idea of God must deepen and deepen within us, and we must not take for granted that we *know* God. For example, every Bible says that it is given by God. Every Holy Book of every nation from South America to India, to here, to there, everyone of them says, "This is God."

For example we say, "God is love." Of course God is love, but what is love? God is light.... You see, we deceive ourselves and *play* with these words, feeling that we know God. Until we understand that we are really in self-deception and are kidding ourselves, we will not really penetrate into the *real meaning* of what God is. *God is understood not by knowing but by becoming.*

Another method to find God and know what God is is to look inside yourself. I do not know any human being who yet knows himself. If you know your Self, you will know *Him*. Science knows about stomachs, kidneys, bones, etc. to a certain degree, but it does not know what is *behind* them, *beyond* them.

Another way in which you can deepen your understanding about the idea of God is *direct experiences — real psychic experiences.* "I heard a voice, and the voice said so and so." Was that really God? We now have five thousand mediums channeling "God." Is it really God they are channeling? The proof that it is not God is that they are all contradicting each other. How can I be sane if I say within half an hour two hundred different things, conflicting things?

If you examine the channeled literature, you will discover that a person with a Ph.d. can write better things.

There was a doctor living in Phoenix who said, "I am receiving masterpiece messages from God." I said, "That is wonderful if it is so, but do not kid yourself. Be a little careful." He brought the pages and we sat down and I read them. I said, "You are a medical doctor?" "Yes." "O.K., I will give you a topic to write about." "What is it?" he asked. "Write about peace." He wrote about peace for half an hour. Then we compared what "God" gave to him and what he wrote. His writing was much more advanced and organized than what he received. I said to him, "You are deceiving yourself."

Do not deceive yourself! If it is God, okay, but prove it. If it is not God, you are really in danger.

Now we are coming to the hundred names of God. One day a Holy man, a Sufi, came and said, "I am going to teach you a hundred names of God." I asked, "God has a hundred names?" He said, "No. In reality, He is the Nameless One. But man can approach Him through various names. We will sit and meditate on each one. In one hundred days we can expand our consciousness in such a way that eventually we can make a contact with that Infinite Presence."

And it was so true. When I started to recite and meditate on these one hundred names year after year, I saw that something very important happened. The bars of the prison in which I was living evaporated. It was as if I were in contact with God every minute. I could talk to Him, ask and receive things from Him. He became Solar, Cosmic, Galactic, Infinite, Something! I do not know yet what He is. If there is any person who can stand up and say, "I know God," I will think that he is lying. No one *knows* God, except someone whose name will be revealed later.

Many philosophers have given names to God. One of these names is *That*. It does not mean anything. For example, in the *Upanishads* it says, "From *That* everything proceeded and to *That* everything will return." What is that *That*? Of course it is very profound, but it does not say anything to **us**. There is no identification, no definition, no characterization — just *That!*

Someone else said, "It is Tao." When asked, "What is Tao?" he replied, "Nothing can be said about It." "Then, why are you calling It Tao?" People have written millions of books about these things. Why say It is Tao if nothing can be known about It?

The next person says, "I am That I am." Again, this is very profound, but what is he saying? Explain to me — I am That I am. Other philosophers say, "God is AUM." What? A-U-M. The people who say this have written many volumes of explanation. AUM. God is the AUM. It does not mean anything to me. Does it mean anything to you? Still others say, "It is the Innermost Self." What is It? Where is It? The Innermost Self . . . .

We are really in a mist. We do not know what God is. But He exists. I think the only way we can have a *good path* toward Him is through transforming ourself, purifying ourself, and making ourself Light, Love, Beauty, and Goodness to such a degree that we become a better mirror to reflect the mystery of God.

That is why Christ once said some very mysterious words, "Those who have seen Me have seen God." This is very beautiful. Is it really true? Well, you think about it.

Sometimes in these pages you will feel a little uneasy because crystallizations in your mind must be slowly destroyed to open the mind to greater visions and dimensions.

We have made God commonplace. Everybody swears about Him. Everybody is "saved" by Him. Everybody imposes Him on each other without knowing what they are doing.

Now, the Sufis gave one hundred names to Him. Look at how beautiful they are.

The Compassionate One

1

He is *the Compassionate One* — the Compassion. It is so beautiful. I cannot find a better name to call Him. Compassion is an unconditional, all-inclusive love. Yesterday I was meditating and collecting my mind to see really what compassion means. In this level, compassion means to have a state of consciousness in which He identifies Himself with every life form.

Compassion has power over the Law of Karma. If for some reason He wants to free you from your karma, He, through His compassion, frees you from any condition or limitation. It is compassion that, like a magnet, draws to Him every speck of life in Cosmos.

Compassion is called the Highest Law. All other laws are formulated by the Law of Compassion to lead the forms of life to their destination. This law shows interest in every atom in manifestation and in every form of life in Existence.

All laws end in compassion. This is why compassion is an open door to contact the Most High.

To have compassion means to be in everything, everywhere, as if everything and everywhere is yourself. *Compassion* is why you are in your body, but you are also in every cell. This is why you have compassion toward your nose, toes, organs, etc. You *love* them. You want to keep them as one. *That is compassion!*

Compassion is a state of consciousness which feels at *one* with every life-form or with the *essence* of every life-form. He is *compassionate*, the Compassionate. Think about it. That gives us a clue that because God feels that He is one with me, then I have a chance to grow into Him.

The All Merciful One

God is *merciful — the All Merciful One*. Who knows why, how, and when we fail, but He has mercy upon us never the less. We made Him a judge and policeman. We say: "If you do this, He will kill you, boil you, burn you." But we cannot do *anything* to change His mercy toward us.

When I visited an asylum, I found many young girls and boys who had "flipped out." It was a pitiful sight. They would have two or three minutes of sanity, then "flip out" again. I talked to a psychiatrist there and asked, "What is happening to them?" He said, "Most of these patients came here because they have guilt complexes. They think that when they die, God will throw them in Hell where they will burn forever and forever, amen." These poor people could not cope with this thought. They needed to know one thing — that *God is merciful*. See how the Sufis bring out the deeper meanings of life?

Of course God is beyond mercy, beyond compassion, because compassion and mercy are words with which we are "playing" to build the "Universe," like the two boys mentioned earlier. But at least these words are giving a little orientation to us.

The King

3

He is *the King*. This is the assumption that He is the *only One*. There is no second, no third, no fourth — only one God — nothing else. He is organized in such a way that this whole created Universe is functioning under His command. This is our understanding, but is it true? Maybe there is something else that we will discover when we "grow," but it looks like that now.

Recently, I learned something interesting from a television show. Some chickens do not lay their eggs until the mosquitoes hatch because the mosquitoes are food for the chicks. See what an *organized* life this is, if we do not spoil and destroy it?

He is the King, organized everywhere and in everything. This is why Christ said, "Thy will be done on earth as it is in heaven." This means that He is the King. If you sit and think about this, you will find so many deeper and deeper ideas coming from your soul. What is the King? What is the physical King, spiritual King, Cosmic King? He is some Power Who has all the power to orchestrate the whole Existence.

The Holy One
4

He is *the Holy One*. Holy means the only One That cannot be materialized in our concepts. God cannot be divided or separated. If you have a separate "God," you are not really following *God*. If you hate my "God" and I hate your "God," neither of us has a God. Do not deceive yourself. *The Holy One* is in everything and everywhere. People say, "Holy be Your Name." This means, God's name must be unified in *every* living being as the only Holy One!

The Peace

5

God is *the Peace.* This is another name given in the Koran and Sufi literature. He is the Peace — *Absolute Bliss, Harmony.* The Peace. Can you imagine? Think about it! We say that when a person has peace, he has some contact with *Him.* These names are signs that you have contact with *Him.*

I believe that ninety-nine percent of all human beings do not have peace. Do you have peace? You are feeling just wonderful, happy, and at peace. Then taxes or something else comes to your mind and your peace is gone. What is that Peace which refers to Him?

If you strive to be a peaceful person, you will understand Him better. If you try to be a king of your own "kingdom," you will be closer to understanding what He is. If you become compassionate, you will understand Who He is. If you are merciful, you will have a little idea of What He is. By cultivating these virtues within ourselves, we open telephone lines to *That Infinite Presence.* Peace — think about that Peace!

Do you have peace? If you have five percent peace, you know Him five percent, but most of us do not have even one percent peace. We panic when fear strikes. Like a poison, fear penetrates our whole system. Where there is fear, there is no peace. Some people think that peace means to store armaments and cheat each other. This is not peace.

Peace is transformation into God. Imagine a large piece of charcoal, one portion of which is fire; that portion is Peace. *When the whole piece of charcoal is fire, you are accepted unto Him. You have peace. You are peace.*

The Faithful

The Faithful. We say, "I know what faithfulness is." Do you really? It is so difficult to find a faithful person. *Faithful* means He never forsakes you, no matter what happens. He never betrays you.

To God we belong and to Him is our return.

— Koran

Faithfulness means you live in Him, you think in Him, you feel in Him, you act in Him. He is your Innermost Self.

The Guardian

The Guardian. Within this concept of God, what does it mean to *guard?* To guard yourself means to reveal Himself within you and through you. To guard means to lead you to your True Self — the God within you.

He does not hold your hand and take you to this church, that church or tell you to read this Bible, that Bible. Man failed to live according to the Holy Books. See what is happening in the world today. People are almost eating each other, destroying each other. Crime is increasing. Deception, exploitation, turmoil, and corruption are increasing up to our throats. Why is that if we really *know* God? We are kidding ourselves.

God is the *faithful Guardian.* What does He do? If you say, for example, "God is my Guardian," that is wonderful! Have you accepted this? "Yes." Then follow His attributes.

Guardian means that He is revealing Himself within you and changing your self into Himself. If you start changing toward God — becoming God's friend and co-worker — then you are guarded, guided.

If you surrender yourself to Him, He will guide you to the Source of Light, Beauty, Love, and Power. He will protect you so you can stay on the path of Beauty and be a Beauty.

The Mighty One

The Mighty One. Can you find something mightier than Him? We do not know what He is yet, but a little earthquake creates Sedona, another earthquake creates the Grand Canyon, and another earthquake takes our whole civilization and dumps it into the center of fire and burns it. You cannot say to God, "I will show You." What are you going to show Him?

There are even people who say, "He does not know what He is doing." It is so interesting. Because people were very frustrated in trying to know God and they could not, they created an insane expression, "God is dead." This solved their problem because God "was dead." Really? Ten or fifteen ministers formed a church and named it "God is Dead." This is what they thought because *they* were dead. Whenever one is dead, he thinks that everyone else is dead! This is really true, and God "died" because they themselves were dead.

Mighty. I remember when we had a seven point earthquake in California. Immediately following the quake, a national news commentator said, "God is mighty. He can do anything He wants." Of course He is mighty, but what do we learn if He is mighty? *We learn that we must never be arrogant and think that we are something. Every human being who thinks that he is something powerful and can do anything he wants denies and slanders God.* Look around you. If you see people around you who think that they are more powerful than God, that their money can move the Universe, or that their position can destroy anything they choose, they are ungodly people. There is no God in them. The mightiness of God makes me extremely humble because I know how powerful He is.

The Compeller

9

The Compeller, One Who forbids things that prevent you from being ready to unify with Him completely. This has a very deep meaning. I was searching through my papers to know what I was thinking at that time. Eventually I brought myself into synthesis and understood that the *Compeller* eradicates all hindrances, obstacles, mental crystallizations, emotional crystallizations, doctrines, and dogmas that separate you from *Him.* For example, a man says, "In the name of God, I must kill you." Or in the name of God, he kills himself because he separated himself from the God Who exists in everything.

If you identify your self with that name, you become invincible and no barrier will stand between you and Him.

The Dignified

The Dignified. Dignity is the result of knowing that the Light of God shines in you and in your face. You think and feel and act in a way that your dignity increases because the Light of God transforms you.

If you meditate on this name, you will cultivate solemnity within you and will develop the sense of His presence. You will grow into the Dignity of God.

The Creator

11

He is called *the Creator*. We take for granted that God created everything, but it is not that easy. Think about it. What does *Creator* mean? If you take a flower and think about it for one year, you are still short of answers. How did He create a flower? Of course we can now create artificial flowers, but this is self-deception. One day I saw my eyes in the mirror and said, "Wow. How did you do this, God? It is really something. They see colors, movements, motions, sizes, forms, everything." Creative!

I was nine years old when my father said, "Did you know that we are in space?" "No," I said, "we are on the earth." "But, the earth is in space," he said. "There is nothing holding the earth?" I asked. He said, "No, it is in the air. It is like a big ball that you throw up and it stays there." "Oh, I'm scared then. Is nothing holding us?" "No. Nothing is holding us," he said.

The whole Universe is in Space. What an intelligent and great wisdom that One must have to make all these billions and billions of stars and orchestrate them like a symphony. Wowee!

The Constructor

God is *the Constructor*. He constructs. See the architectural phenomena of Nature. One day a great Sage explained to me how the stars turn and balance and interpenetrate each other without touching the rhythms of each other to form a great framework. This is only one Solar System, one Galaxy. What about all Galaxies together? *See what He constructed — the trees, the birds, the flowers! You!* Your existence is within all of His existence.

The Fashioner

The Fashioner. If you want to know what a *real* fashioner is, you think about God. There are no two human beings who are exactly alike. See the variety of things. Even a leaf is unique. No two leaves are alike. What mind is that, what creativity, what power is that? The Hindus say, "He sang and everything came into manifestation."

We must feel that knowing about the names of God is a very serious matter. *God exists, and we must try to get in contact with Him and go closer to Him.* To go closer to Him does not mean to pray only and read books only. It means slowly to be like Him. You can be like Him if you understand these names and try to be them.

The Motionless One

The Motionless One. He is *Motionlessness* in all motion. He is *action in all inactivity.* Can you imagine what it is like to be motionless in all the noise around you? Can you quiet yourself from the physical noises, the emotional noises, the mental noises?

Go out into Nature. Sit quietly near the ocean, on the mountains, and be motionless. This is what Great Teachers did. They went to the forests and they meditated years and years to penetrate into the secrets of creation. They were not like us, sitting in front of the television, eating and drinking all the obnoxious things given to us. They were in seclusion and meditation. It is so interesting.

The Conqueror

The Conqueror. Those who are more God and less human are those who will conquer. There was a king who was the enemy of Buddha. He collected five thousand of Buddha's disciples and killed them. Then he tried various ways and means to kill Buddha. Buddha said, "You cannot fight against a man who is enlightened," which means closer to God.

The king started to do everything possible to kill Buddha. Then one day, he found that his whole body was swollen like a pig's. At the same time he heard a voice say, "In a few days you will pass away." The king said, "I must go to Buddha and confess." So the king went before that man Who had nothing else but a shirt. Buddha said, "I forgive you. Now go and live a decent life and do not fight against Light." He conquered the king. This king became one of those who collected many, many manuscripts of the Teacher and published them. *God always conquers.*

Those who are with God and walk with God will be the future conquerors of the Universe.

The Best Bestower

The Best Bestower. This means He shares everything He is and He has — air, sunshine, water, everything that is growing, everything that is beautiful. He shares; He bestows. Can we be like Him?

People see only those gifts that are visible. What about the treasures of our mind, of our soul, of the Space, of invisible worlds, the everlasting life . . . ?

We must turn into a flame of gratitude that He bestows to us, not only the finite but also the Infinite.

The Sustainer
17

The Sustainer. This is very important. He sustains His Presence in *everything*. Think about it! Sustainer.

He is the Sustainer of all powers of the Universe, of all Beings — visible and invisible, of all galaxies and constellations, and of all That is in them.

How much your consciousness expands when you think that He meets the needs of all Life.

The Opener

18

The Opener. This is very mysterious. I was asking, "What does He open?" He opens the gates and windows that lead you to Himself.

Opener. The mind is open now. Wow! For example, people create a mess by attaching to this person, to that person, to that religion, to that faith. When they are opened, they understand. To be *opened* means the destruction of all crystallizations, prejudices, and superstitions built day and night in our minds that we are the "only way to fly."

He opens the bars of our minds, emotions, and habitats and releases us toward His freedom. He gives freedom to your Spirit.

The Knower

The Knower. He knows. In the *Holy Book* it says, "He knows before you think what you are going to think. He knows what you are going to do before you do it." *He knows.* In the Psalms it says He knows when you are in the womb of your mother what you are going to do. He knows because all your past deeds and karma are computerized in front of Him. *He knows.*

Q&A

Question: In The Great Invocation where it says, "seal the door where evil dwells," how does that relate to God as a Sustainer of everything?

Answer: Not everything! He does not sustain diseases, vices, animosity, hatred. He sustains His Presence within you. This is very secret language. It may slip past your ears. He sustains Light, Love, and Beauty.

That verse in The Great Invocation[1] means different things. For example, if I say, "May your disease be sealed and finished," it means you no longer have the disease. Or if I say, "May these crimes be sealed, may these wars and hatreds be stopped," the door is sealed. It is finished. *Seal* is a very secret language. It means to make something inactive — powerless — because nothing can be destroyed in the world except all those things that prevent you from reaching Him.

Question: Isn't everything that happens to us the Will of God?

---

1. See back of book for full text.

Answer: I knew you would get me . . . . You see, the Will of God cannot operate in you unless you make it operate. So, it means that if something is happening to you, it is your own choice. In *Dialogue With Christ* I told about a young neighbor boy who came to me and said, "I hate God." "You do?" I said. "What did God do to you?" "My friend Paul was running across the street when a car ran over his head and killed him. What kind of God is this?" In his Sunday School he was told that nothing happens except by the Will of God, so he was taking God to court.

I had a very difficult time with him. I told him how some people are victims of negative emotions and mental disorders. Things happen because of karma and mental disorders, and also when people do not stand up for their rights. Then I started to explain to him the Law of Karma. He said, "Now I can understand and love God." This really happened.

Then I said, "God, did I do something wrong by pacifying that boy and creating peace and joy in him by speaking about the Law of Incarnation and Karma?" In the 14th Century they would have hanged me for such a statement.

It is your karma, it is your action that is fulfilled. Whatever you have wanted, it has happened to you. Do not blame God for everything you do. If it is the will of God, let us give a chance to every criminal to come and kill us. Some oriental nations believe this. For example, if someone destroys them they say,

"God wanted it." Why are they not saying that they were so stupid they could not defend themselves?

It was 1914 when the Ottoman Turks began to collect male Armenians, sixteen to forty-five years old, and send them to build the highways, then slaughter them. A few months later they collected 45,000 Armenians and in a few weeks time slaughtered them. They slaughtered them in groups of 5,000 and 2,000, leading them into the wilderness and then shooting them or killing them with daggers. The clergymen and priests were with them, and they advised the people not to resist but to obey "the will of God." Suddenly a woman shouted, "The will of God is *not* the will of evil," and she was shot immediately by the police.

For a long time the genocide of two million people haunted me day and night. I could not understand how a compassionate God could do all these things that happened and are happening in the world today. Genocide is going on in many places, and no one stops this "will of God." The real Will of God was given by Moses when He said, *"Do not kill."*

God is the One Self. In Him we live, act, and have our being. In the essence of man, God is. We have within us all the essence of our Father. He lives in us just as an earthly father lives within us through his genes.

God is transcendental. He is beyond the visible and invisible Universe, but also he is within us. All that exists is in Him.

The highest morality and liberation or salvation of humanity is based on one supreme fact — that the manifested Universe has One Self and the One Self is within all of us. If we think and speak enough about the One Self, all suffering and pain will disappear from the earth.

The Law of the One Self is the One Law. The One Self is the Law. All transgressions in our lives are transgressions against the One Self, the One Law. All laws in heaven and earth are branches of this One Law. All forms, all powers will eventually recognize the Oneness of the Self — the All-Self.

The higher integrity of a person is built upon this Law. This Law is the fountainhead of all streams, of all laws.

Any law or action against this Law is a source of suffering, is an action against one's own future.

We do not need armies and ammunitions. We need only to spread all over the world the existence of the One God — the existence of the One Self.

So, in talking about the names of God we did not insult or limit Him. What did we do? We expanded His majesty in our minds. Try to think about these names of God so that you can understand the next ones.

Whatever good happens to thee is from God, but whatever will happen to thee is from thy own soul.

This is one of the most profound statements in the Koran. Meditate upon it.

When we say "one hundred names of God," does it mean we are defining God or giving a definition of God with these hundred names? No. It is impossible. God cannot be defined. It is beyond our imagination, our visualization, our thinking, but the names given in Sufi literature are the powers of God — the radiations of God.

Let us say that we have a sun, and the sun's rays are coming to us. Each ray is one power, one name. A hundred rays are coming from that Central Power. Each ray is different, but also it is the sun. Each ray is one with the sun. We must not think that by knowing these names, we are knowing Him. It is impossible to know *Him.*

Thinking and talking about these names does something very mysterious to us, and that is what the Sufis intended to do. When you are thinking about His names and really meditating upon them, speaking about them, analyzing and brooding over them, the power that is within you, the corresponding power of those names within you is activated. You can start becoming divine by thinking about divine attributes. As you think more deeply about divine attributes, divine powers, divine beauty, and divine grace, as well as about the names that are supposedly His names, the corresponding points within you that are latent or dormant begin to awaken. You feel that by thinking and talking about these names you are progressing on the Path of return toward your Self.

Each of these one hundred names is a technique to make people God-conscious. Your geometry, algebra does not do that. Your science does not do that. Your politics does not do that. Your education cannot do that. But if you start thinking about the attributes and aspects, about the names and powers of God and His laws, slowly you will see that you are Him because the corresponding qualities will begin to unfold within you. This is the secret behind discussing these names.

In many Sufi monasteries I have seen great Teachers sit for one day, two days, three days, four days with 107 or 120 beads in their hands. They say the names of God. For example they say, "Yalatif," which means *the Beauty,* and they think, "Beauty. Wow. What is Beauty?" Then they look at the rivers and the sky and say, "Beauty." Then they go into deep meditation.

You can see how beautiful they are. They are not like preachers who stand there and give you the "ticket to hell." They don't sell tickets to hell. They do not rebuke you. They do not belittle you because they understand that each of you essentially is divine. The greatest secret of education and leadership is to bring that Divinity out of you in such a way that it begins to manifest in everything you are doing, speaking, thinking, and relating to.

If you start meditating on these names, you will see that something is awakening within you and not letting you do things you do not like to do. Why is that? Look at how interesting it is. This is so important. By thinking about these one hundred names, the aspects and attributes or powers and laws of God, you begin to control your own mechanical side. You become a conscious human being. When you see that your mechanical side wants to interfere and do things, speak things, think things, and feel things, you have now a little power, a little control over them and can intervene and force your own will on the automatic side of yourself. This is all we can do to control the automatic side of ourselves which is always activated through posthypnotic suggestions and subconscious urges and drives.

Sit for five or ten minutes and ask yourself, "Am I doing things, speaking things, feeling things, and thinking things with my own will, or are different energies, forces, influences doing what I am doing? You will be surprised! Most of the time you do things without knowing why you do them. It is very interesting.

Let us continue with the names of God.

One Who Expands

One Who Expands. When you think about God, you slowly realize that there is no limit to expansion. When you make contact with Him, you start expanding. Limitations break within you. Personal consciousness seems to survive through limitations. Whatever you do you are limiting yourself, you are limiting others, or limiting things in order to understand them. When you contemplate about God or his names, you gradually break your limitations. He is the power that extends and spreads.

When we physically do something, it goes eternally into Space. We never think that these words we are speaking now are going to the Galaxies. They are gone already. They travel faster than the light. Do you see how interesting it is to think that God is a Power that extends, spreads, and we are the same?

Everything that exists has no limit, has no limitations. Your words, your thoughts, your emotions, your deeds are already in the computer. They are everywhere, in everything. For example, A great Sufi Teacher once said, "At the time of judgment, your shoes and clothes will stand as witnesses to what you were doing when you were wearing them." They will say, "Hey, I saw him!" One or two hundred years ago this philosophy would have seemed really stupid. But if you think about it today, it is so interesting. Your voice, your emotions, your deeds are impressed in everything, everywhere. There is no escape!

We are doing only a few minutes of meditation by speaking about these things here, but what will happen if we sit and think about *limitlessness?* Does anything have a limit? It does not. It goes bigger, bigger, bigger, bigger. It goes smaller, smaller, smaller. And bigger and smaller are mixed. Then they come down again. They circle and circle, becoming smaller and bigger, smaller and bigger . . . . There is no end to smallness and bigness.

So you are going to think about the limitlessness of God. That is *Him*. But then you will notice one thing. As you think about God as a limitless *something*, you will start thinking about you — yourself — that you are also limitless. Now what happened? The limitlessnesses fused, or the mechanism there started to become reactivated within you. You are becoming a little more in tune with that Highest Power or Lowest Power or Largest Power or Smallest Power — these words are all stupid words. It is one thing. Do you understand that? And that is one of the names of God, the twentieth name.

The Abaser — The Humiliator

21

The Abaser — the Humiliator. God humiliates you. God humiliates everything. Why? He is so out there.... He is so great, so glorious, so big, so limitless that in front of Him you feel humiliated. You feel total humiliation. And when you become more and more humiliated, eventually you come to a point of consciousness in which you see that humiliation is nothing else but identification with your divine nature which is looking at your personality.

Suddenly you are humiliated so much that you break that level and start being like Him. The deeper you go into Him, the more people will feel humiliated in your presence. They will feel smaller and smaller. This is what you feel when you see a great Teacher.

A great Teacher visited our monastery one day. When He sat on the chair, my gosh! I felt just like a little mosquito. He gave a five minute talk, and my mind went everywhere. A moment came when I felt I was going "crazy." My mind stopped in His presence. He was so big.

So, always, Glory imposes humiliation upon you, but this is not a humiliation of your Divinity. The short-comings, the weaknesses, the failures which you are identified with are humiliated in front of your Divinity. Did you see that? It is so beautiful. Now, just the opposite name comes.

The Exalter

The Exalter. He exalts you. To be exalted means to feel, deeper and deeper, that you are immortal, you are everlasting, you are a jewel, you are very precious, you are His son, His daughter, you are His friend, you are His co-worker, you are His companion. The Exalter! And whoever gets closer to God is exalted. How? As you go closer to Him, you resign from the most stupid things with which you were identified. You leave them behind and behind and behind. As you leave behind your failures, stupidities, insanities, obnoxious things, attachments, you become exalted, exalted, exalted, exalted. Do you see how beautiful it is?

How can you exalt others? In reality, you cannot *do* anything except *be something and influence their life. That is all.* If you are exalted, you do not need any plan, any structure, any blueprint to make people exalted because your *presence* is enough for them.

Once, a great Teacher and his two disciples were traveling. The Teacher said, "Let us go through this village bazaar." The disciples said, "What will we say?" "We'll see," said the Teacher. They solemnly and beautifully passed through the multitudes at the bazaar. Everyone was worshiping and respecting them. After they passed through the village one of the disciples asked, "Master, we didn't say anything." He replied, "Didn't you see how the people were elevated, exalted, in heaven because they saw us? They saw how rhythmic, beautiful, influential, and imposing was our spirituality, our Divinity." One of the names of God is the Exalter!

If you do not feel that exaltation, you are not progressing. And if you are not exalting others, you are not progressing because whatever you are, the same thing you will do for others. Of course there is a time-period where people fight with themselves, with their difficulties and limitations until they break through and the higher influence starts penetrating into them.

The Strengthener

The Strengthener — the One Who makes you stronger. Who can make you stronger than God can? In the lives of many saints, many heroes, and many martyrs in Christianity, Islam, Buddhism, Hinduism, Zoroastrianism, in politics, education, and science, all who became stronger and stronger were those who walked with God. He makes you stronger because as you think about Him, you become like Him to a certain degree. You are getting closer. He is a Sun and you are a candle, but you have Light now, and the Light will increase, increase, increase.

He can be your courage, your daring, your striving. He can strengthen your intellect, your love, your enthusiasm, your fire, your willpower, your purity. He can also strengthen your self renunciation.

The Dishonorer

The Dishonorer. He makes you dishonored because if you stand in His Light, you suddenly see how obnoxious you are. Did you have that experience? Close your eyes and stand in front of your God. See what will happen. It is as if millions of volts of light are upon you, and everything is seen in you from A to Z. Physical defects, emotional defects, mental defects are projected on the wall of the screen, and you see yourself. Wow! What is this? It is trash. When you think about this, it makes you so beautiful because the first step toward the greater wisdom is a realization of your failures, mistakes, and stupidities. Unless you realize these things, you are a blind and deaf person and you cannot proceed on the Path.

I have met many, many people. The first thing I ask, "How do you feel?" They reply, "Oh, excellent." "How is your spiritual life?" "It is tops." There is no hope for them. They are finished. They know everything, they are everything, they are "pure." They are already living in the wings of God as "mosquitoes." Do you see? There is no hope. But if someone comes and says, "I am lost. I do not know what to do. I want to do right things, but I am doing wrong. I read and pray and go to church, but I am just a low rascal of a human being." There is great hope for this person because he has started to see what he is.

That is why Socrates said, "Know thyself." Exactly know what you are.

Do not say that you are a great person, a holy person, a saint, this or that. Only criminals and insane people think they are great, that they are at the top. But sane people see things exactly as they are. No one is condemning you. You are going to see it and then feel dishonored in front of Him. Sometimes you must stand in the Light of your Solar Angel and say, "Look at me, look at me now. What do You see?" Oh, what He sees! Let Him not say what He sees!

But it is good to see it. Let us say that you are going to take your car on an important journey, but you do not know about the defects in your car. You are in great danger. The same is true on the spiritual path. Unless you check your "car" and find all the defects you have and repair them, you cannot run on the freeway of spirituality.

You see, I noticed this in my life. A moment came when I was going to do a very advanced meditation, samadhi, contemplation. I said, "I can do it." Then suddenly I saw what was happening to me.

I can explain to you how it happens. Let us say that the tires of your car are out of balance. When you drive around the city at ten to fifteen miles per hour, you do not feel it. Your car is perfect. It is leaking a little, but it is all right. It is making little noises, here, there, but that is all right because it is not giving you trouble. OK. Now go on the freeway at ninety miles per hour. Wow.... The tires are vibrating, the oil leaks more and more, and the temperature is going up. The noise that you thought was something little became a big crack somewhere in the engine. Then suddenly your car either explodes or stops. But it did not happen when you were in the city!

When you are not advanced spiritually, your defects do not come to the surface. When you advance, small bugs hidden here and there come to the surface and tell you, "Hey. What are you doing? You did not repair your car, and now you are driving ninety miles per hour!" You feel dishonored. Do you see what I am saying?

All-Knowing

All-knowing. All-knowing is one of His names. All-knowing, Omniscient, All-knowingness. He knows what is happening to you. Do you see how beautiful it is to think about this name? While you are thinking about this name, some transformation is happening in your consciousness. What is happening? Let us see. I am thinking that He can hear everything. All-hearing. He can hear everything. So whatever I am saying, He is hearing. Does He hear also my thoughts? Yes. Does He hear my feelings? Yes. If He hears, then what am I going to do? I am going to behave. That is the change. Do you see how you change yourself, your behavior, in thinking about Him and how He always hears you? You will be careful what you say to your loved ones, to your friends, to the people around you.

In thinking about this attribute, about the name of God, you come to your senses. Sit and say, "All-hearing God, do You hear *everything*?" "Yes...." "If You are hearing everything, what am I going to do?" Your Soul will say, "From now on, zip your mouth or know exactly what you are saying because He is hearing it." It is very beautiful.

All-Seeing One

All-seeing One. When I went to a temple in Asia, on the altar there was a big eye — one eye. It was so interesting. I stood in front of it and looked. It was painted so beautifully that it penetrated everywhere in my nature. When I went this way, it was looking at me. When I went that way, it was looking at me. I went down, it is looking. I went up, it is looking — the all-seeing eye.

Now what is happening? Again, if He sees everything, you can no longer play hide-and-seek. What are you going to do? Either you are going to imagine that He cannot see anything and you can do anything you want, or you are going to know that He *sees*, and now you do not have a choice because He sees.

Do you see how the names, the attributes change your consciousness and your relationship with yourself and with others? And these are only a few words about the names. What if you took those hundred names and thought for one week on each name or for one year on each name? Then you would live one hundred years.

Somebody did it. "God," he said, "Look. I am going to be a good boy." God asked, "What are you going to do?" "Until I finish meditating on Your names, do not take my soul." And God promised! When the man came to the ninety-ninth name, he said, "How would it be if I started from the beginning?" God said, "No, just finish it." Yes, there are some comic stories like that.

The Judge

27

He is *the Judge*. In Sufi literature the word "judge" has a different meaning from our common understanding. According to Sufi philosophy God never judges. Our religion, our Western civilization is built upon judgment. Open your newspapers. See your television. Listen to your radio. From beginning to end, it is judgment, judgment, judgment. But *judgment* in reality means karma. *In karma you judge yourself because you are God within you.* God is not going to sit and read the personal files of ten billion people as they pass in front of Him. What a stupid business is that! I would not do it.

But when you start seeing yourself as you are, you will judge yourself. And what will be your judgment? From the Western viewpoint, judgment means to humiliate and condemn yourself. But in *real* philosophy, judgment or karma means to find ways and means to raise yourself to a state of consciousness where you can no longer sow the seeds of cause and effect. You have passed that. It is so beautiful!

But here in our churches, "God" condemns you. You are going to hell. You are dirty sinners and so on. Well, people became greater and greater sinners when we told them they are sinners. Tell them that they are Gods, and they will be like Gods because they are really. In essence they are!

God's judgment is to shine His Light on you so that you see what you were, are, and will be. His judgment is to give you an opportunity to come to your senses and follow His Path.

Righteousness

Righteousness. Righteousness means that nothing will happen to you unless you wanted it to happen to you. It is so interesting. Righteousness is the answer to what you do — good or bad.

Righteousness is unification with God. Think about that. Righteousness? What is righteousness? And are you righteous? Are people righteous? What do we need to be righteous, and what things must we eliminate to be righteous? Can we really be closer to God without righteousness? Why is righteousness important? Think about it!

He is righteous in all His actions toward you and me because He knows what you are, what you do, what you feel, what you think. One can be righteous when He is all-knowing.

 The Beauty

The Beauty. God's name is Beauty. Whenever you see any beauty, think that God is there.

Worship God in any form of beauty. Do not separate God from beauty. See or discover beauty within yourself, within others. Search for beauty, and when you find it think that you talked to God.

Beauty is everywhere in human actions, feelings, thoughts, visions. You can find many fields of beauty.

See the beauty in wisdom, in the arts, in the drops of tears, in smiles. See beauty in the power of Nature. In seeing beauty and appreciating beauty, you get closer to Beauty.

The Aware One

The One Who is aware of everything in everything. To be aware of everything .... That is nothing yet, but the next part is really intricate. He is aware of everything **in everything**.

When Saint Francis of Assisi was talking to the birds and giving a sermon to them, people asked him, "What are you doing?" He said, "Well, I am talking to the birds so that they progress on the spiritual path." They said, "This man is crazy." Then there was another great Saint who used to go and sit near the trees and talk to them. He would say, "Look, you are eventually going to be like this, ... like this." See, he was talking to them.

These great Saints were imagining and realizing that God is in everything, that He is aware in everything. The chair you are sitting on now is aware of what you are. Your clothes are aware because God is there also. Can you tell me where God is not? You cannot. That is the mystery.

In the Psalms there is a very beautiful expression which says, "If I go to heaven, You are there. If

I go to hell, You are there. Where can I escape from You?"

Can you escape? Think about awareness in everything everywhere. It is so beautiful.

Awareness is absolute consciousness.

The Patient One

The Patient One. I once saw a great Teacher repeating this name maybe a thousand times and thinking about it. The Patient One. Then I saw, really, how patient that man was. You could do almost anything in his presence. He would just look at you. Then you would come slowly to your senses. He did not do anything but look at you.

One day some men stole three goats from our school. We went immediately to this Teacher and said, "They stole the goats. What do we do now?" "Well, he said, we will think about it." I said, "We are going to take guns and chase them." "That is one of the ways to do it," he said, "but be patient and they will come back."

Now listen very carefully. And the Teacher closed his eyes. "Be patient," he said. "They will come back." What was he doing? He went spiritually to them and said, "Bring the goats back."

One day. They didn't come. Two days. They didn't come. Three days . . . . Finally I went to him and said, "Teacher, the goats are still not here." "Be patient, be patient," he said.

Four days later the two men came, shot and wounded, seeking refuge and healing in the school. The Teacher said, "Where are the goats?" The goats came later. Do you see? He was patient.

Patience is *action* in the spiritual plane. When you shut down all activities in the personality, your Soul starts to act. This is *patience*, but how to explain these things . . . .

The Magnificent

32

The Magnificent. Think about it. I like this name very much. Think about each other as magnificent people. What a change will happen in your consciousness!

Eighty percent of humanity think of each other as the most pitiful, obnoxious human beings. No matter in what ways you humiliate your partners, the people you work with or live with, you are looking down on them. But what will happen if you think that *the Magnificent* is living in each of them? The Magnificent! It is beyond imagination. "Magni" means the Great.

The Forgiver

The Forgiver. It is so bad that in some literature they think that God is revengeful. He kills and destroys, sees your sins, steps on your neck, and takes you to a hell where you are finished and condemned forever.

In Sufi literature God is the Forgiver. Look what is happening. If He does not forgive, He is defeating His Divinity. How can He allow a portion of Himself to be lost? It is only forgiveness that makes that portion achieve the highest.

Forgiveness is a *secret* and that secret is this: *You forgive someone when you accept that his failures are yours.* You cannot forgive anything if you do not feel that. In *The Upanishads* it says, "The good things you did, I did. The bad things you did, I did, so do not let me do bad things."

How much are you going to develop that forgiveness? No matter what you do, forgive it. Forgiveness. If one feels that all the failures of others are his, he slowly learns to forgive them.

All this literature that is written about a revengeful God, a destroying God, the Guide to Hell.

Look at what bad names we gave to God! But His real name is the Forgiver. Just like an ocean — you throw something in it and ten days later it is all washed clean. It is finished. Who are you that you can spoil God? With all your obnoxiousness, He is the Forgiver. You always have a chance to be His friend.

If we develop this forgiveness in our politics, in our courts, what a change will happen! But can we do that? It is almost impossible. We condemn ourselves to death because we love death.

You see, when you do not forgive, you feel that you "exist." And one of the traps of the human being is to feel that you exist, that you are something, somebody. If you forgive you feel that you have lost something, your dignity, your power. To replace this feeling of emptiness, you attach to vices, to negativity to feel that you exist. Your control is lost, and you don't want to lose your ego. But lose your ego so that your soul comes into being. That is too heavy, isn't it!

The more you forgive, the closer you go to Him. Forgiveness eventually annihilates your ego and vanity.

Gratitude

God is *Gratitude.* This is a most beautiful one. I love this one. Those who are grateful are closer to God because gratitude is an appropriation of Life and its laws. Also, God Himself, we suppose, is grateful for all progress that is going on in all Galaxies. Everything is progressing in the ocean of His gratitude. His gratitude is like a magnet which pulls up all seeds of Life to Himself.

Do you know that? You see, when you are talking about gratitude, you are talking about Him. He is *the Gratitude.* You need two or three months to think, to penetrate into the meaning.

Gratitude.... Everything is beautiful, everything is in order. Everything will be in order. There is the highest respect for every seed of light. He is gratitude. If you do something obnoxious, He is the gratitude. If you do something good, He is the gratitude because no matter what you do, your wrong things and right things will lead you to the same spot. One way is painful. The other is joyful. That is the only difference.

The Sublime

35

The Sublime. This is beyond our imagination and visualization. It is Infinity, infiniteness. That is another name. I don't know what to say about it. It is Grandeur. It is Power. It is Something.

By thinking on this name you activate a process of sublimation in you. You see your ugliness and you try to purify and beautify yourself.

The names of God are given to challenge us to cultivate them in our beingness and life.

Akbar – the Great

Akbar — the Great. This is very interesting. The Great, Great, Great. You can see His greatness when you look at the stars, when you imagine how man is created, how man thinks and speaks and sees and hears. What a magnificent power and intellect created all that is.

When you start thinking that in every human being the seed of Greatness is there, you will change your whole attitude.

"Destroy them! Release an atomic bomb and get rid of them. They are not thinking as we do; destroy them." You cannot do those things because the Greatness is in **everyone**.

How to arrange things so that Greatness always comes to the surface in spite of the trash which is on the surface.

Greatness is developed in us through the actualization of love.

The Preserver

The Preserver is another name of God. To preserve means to make something continuously exist in spite of all forces against it. God preserves the human soul. He preserves the individuality of the man or the human soul who, as a seed, grows age after age until the God-glory in him reaches its supreme unfoldment.

The Feeder

The Feeder. You are fed physically, emotionally, mentally, and spiritually. Who feeds you? Nature feeds you. The air feeds you. Light feeds you. Ideas feed you. Visions feed you. Power feeds you. Inspiration feeds you. You are fed! Do you see how beautiful it is?

People are not always awake or conscious. Once they come to their senses, they will see that God — the whole Existence — is the Source of abundance on all planes. We live in abundance if we do not deprive each other and pollute the Nature.

The Redeemer

The Redeemer. Stick to Him because He is going to redeem you.

God is the power who redeems those whom He sees striving toward Home, trying to live according to His will. He redeems people by kindling the fires of love toward God . . . and love toward all creation.

Redemption is a process of manifesting God's beauty and His attributes in us. No one can be redeemed except by the power of the Redeemer in him. God redeems people, making them His friends, those who understand His glory and live accordingly.

Q&A

Question: *What do you mean when you say, "to come to your senses?"*

Answer: To come to your senses means to see things as they are now. Do not fabricate things. Do not put colored glasses on your eyes and look at things and say they are blue or they are yellow. Just be clear, direct, and straight. As it is. That means to come to your senses.

For example, if you are drunk, you are not in your senses. When you are angry, you are not in your senses. When you are totally excited, you are not in your senses. Coming to your senses means to cool down, be yourself, and see things as they are. That is what it means to come to your senses.

Cool down. That is very important. Sometimes we must say to each other, "Cool down."

I enjoyed preparing these names and thinking about them. Someday, I will go on a retreat and go over these hundred names for at least three months, fasting and thinking about them. They are so beautiful.

The hundred names of God! What is wrong with it? Recently someone said to me, "People think that you are creating a new God." I said, "God is always *new*." Those who think that God is old do not know

God. God always regenerates Himself. He is always new.

That is another attribute that is not in the names. God is always new. Why new? It is because He is perpetually creative.

> *Question: What do you do when you are caught between two worlds? You are aware that God is watching you, but you do not have the momentum to stop yourself from doing things you do not want to do.*

Answer: Continue thinking about Him. Do not be occupied with your shortcomings and failures and mistakes. Do not think about them.

The psychiatrists, psychologists, our teachers, our ministers, our confessors do something very obnoxious. They say, "Think of how many bad things you have done in the past. Realize them." And you get more and more identified with your failures. You become more obnoxious.

Leave the failures alone. Let them go and think about the *Highest*. Suddenly, the Highest will come like an eagle and take you to the highest peak.

This is the new psychology. The old psychology is dead, but there are millions and millions of new psychological offices opening to say the same thing: "How stupid you are." Well, we know it! I am sick of hearing that I am bad. Can't you tell me something better? Can't you tell me that I am good? "Yes, you are good." Thank God! There is hope now. I can be somebody! By making people condemn themselves, you are killing the Divinity in them. Raise them up and tell them how beautiful they are in spite of failures, etc.

Some husbands belittle and criticize their wives from morning till night. You are dressed wrong, you are walking wrong, you are thinking wrong, you are doing wrong things. Wrong and wrong and wrong. The woman does not know what to do anymore. She is lost. But some women are also like that to their husbands. They pick, pick, pick at them for everything. "You didn't shave, you didn't pick up, you didn't do this or that," and the husband becomes so frustrated that he looks at another woman who praises him.

Why do people want to be praised? I was asking a psychologist this question. He said, "Because they are stupid." I said, "No. In your heart you know that you are something worthy of worship. You want to be praised because you feel that you are divine in spite of all the trash around you." This is the deeper psychology, and this is why every person wants to be respected, loved, praised, exalted, even worshiped.

Once, in a Buddhist temple, I saw the great Teachers come and bow to the students. They said, "We bow to the greatness in you." Imagine what would happen if husbands and wives would do this to each other for two or three days. Either the neighbors would think they were insane, or they will create a new family for themselves.

As we think and meditate upon the names of God, we must always remember that He is within our Innermost Self. These names of God are also the names of the Infinite which lives in man.

As we have seen, one of the names of God is *Beauty*. This and other names connect man to God. As we cultivate beauty in our life, we reveal Him within ourselves and in Him we bloom.

It is very important that we meditate upon the names of God daily and even repeat them often to reinforce the feeling of His Presence within us. By meditating upon and repeating the names of God, we not only develop His attributes within us, but also the names of God become paths for us toward the Infinite. His names become living, life-giving energies within us, and we become charged by Him Who dwells within us.

Not only does He dwell in man, but He is also in every form. In every beauty He is the *Beautiful*. In every knowledge He is the *Knower*. In every love He is the *Compassion*.

As it is impossible to limit Him with names and define Him, it is also impossible to define the Infinity living in man.

His names are words of power. They are challenges for us. They are an invitation for us to develop the attributes of God, to cultivate the essence of the names in our life.

How profound it is to be occupied with the names of God! We say that God has names, but in reality He has no name. How can we define something or give a name to what is nameless and is so great and so big, so deep and so vast that our names cannot fit Him?

Then what are the names? The names are the definitions of our feelings. When we feel something about God in our prayers or meditations or in our contemplative moments, we give that feeling a name — and we call that name "the name of God."

So, it is very interesting that we measure God by our own feelings, or even by our own reason and logic. But He has no names. He is the Nameless One. For example, the Chinese say, "He is the Space. He is the Emptiness."

He has no name. He is in everything, and His name is Everything. It is so beautiful.

But giving Him a name does something important for us. For example, if we say that God is beautiful — the more beautiful we become, the more we become like Him.

The feeling that we have about Him — that He is beautiful — transforms us. As we think and meditate and contemplate about beauty, we slowly become the ideal that we are giving a name to. He is the Beauty.

OK. He is the Beauty. But what does it do for me? If then I become beautiful, I become like Him.

His names are like challenges. And we try to strive to be like the names He has. And being the names that He has, we get closer to His characteristics, to His infinity, to His beauty, to His whatever it is. In giving Him names, we create a challenge for us. For instance, we say that God is the Loving One. If God is the Loving One and if I become a loving one, I become like Him. So, in giving Him names, I challenge myself really to actualize the name that I am giving to Him. It is very interesting.

Also, the names are mantrams. When we give names to God, we put a great power in that name, a great vision, a great Intuition. We do not understand really what that name is because it is the definition of a feeling. It is not reason and logic. That name carries a very powerful energy within itself. Now by repeating that name and thinking about that name, we disclose the capacity of our feeling. And we create a relationship between us and that vision which we have about Him. Repeating the name of God makes us strive toward the meaning of that name, toward the vision of that name, and slowly, slowly we build a procedure for overcoming our limitations and reaching greater heights of understanding and actualization.

The Calculator 40

The Calculator. We have such complicated calculations which are used in astronomy, in mathematics, in physics, in chemistry, and in many other fields of human labor. These calculations are the inventions of human beings who, in comparison to God, are dust atoms. What a great Calculator must exist to manage all that is needed in the whole of Creation, in all kingdoms, to keep control and balance.

The Calculator knows all cycles, all numbers, all symbols, all that happens and will happen everywhere, in everything.

The Ancients told us that He was the Great Architect of the Universe, the Mathematician, the Source of numbers and measures. All human achievements in these fields are drops of His Light.

The Majestic

41

The Majestic. What does majestic mean? It means something so beautiful, so glorious, so beneficent, so deep that we cannot really understand what it is. It is beyond our reason and logic, but it is a feeling. We feel that we cannot define God except by calling Him Majestic.

And what is the Majestic? Majestic is defined and understood according to your level. If you are in the valley, that tree is majestic, but if you are on the mountaintop, that valley is majestic. If you are in higher positions, you can see the sky and the sky is majestic. If you, for example, go to the farthest star and start looking, you will say that that is majestic. It depends on where you are.

Majestic means, first of all, that the feeling you have about Him cannot be defined by your logic and reasoning. But it is something that makes you unfold. That is so beautiful! He is majestic. Well, if He is majestic, you have now in your mind a measure, a standard. If you live a life which is not majestic but ugly and trashy, you will see the difference between you and Him and then try to be majestic like Him.

How majestic is He? He is majestic to the degree that you are unfolded. The more you unfold, the more He is majestic. He is more majestic because you are becoming more majestic. Do you understand that? His name becomes a mysterious magnet that slowly, slowly pulls you out of your limitations and ugliness and slowly makes you majestic. You start talking in majestic ways. You dress in majestic ways. You speak in majestic ways. You deal with people majestically. It is so interesting. But if you do not have as a standard that He is majestic, now that you have some feeling of what majestic means, you can see that you cannot develop toward that majestic Entity.

You yourself create standards for yourself, and those standards which you create about God become a bridge between you and Him. Now, your standards are a little pipe between you and the ocean, but at least you have a communication line. In thinking that He is majestic, you start pulling energy from that Source of Majestic Power.

Majestic also means to have control, to be aware. To control what? To control everything that exists.

Majesty comes from the word mastery — Magi — which means One Who knows and has control.

The Generous One

42

The Generous One. This name is also very beautiful. If you study these words you will see that when religions speak about the virtues, they are speaking about the names of God. Why should we develop virtues? When we develop virtues, we become like Him. At least we approach Him one or two inches. It is better than nothing. At least we approach.

What does it mean to be generous? In these days everything you need must be paid for. You work and work, and sometimes no matter what you do you cannot meet your needs. In addition, you pay taxes on what you receive. You buy your shoes and pay for them. You go to the doctor and get bankrupted. There are lots of things for which you pay and pay and pay, and eventually you are going to be in such a state that you cannot move your feet without paying something.

Look how generous God is. You can look at the stars. You do not pay anything. You see these flowers and bushes and trees and forests, and you do not pay anything unless they have been manipulated and stolen by people to sell you something for which they did not pay.

The air that you are breathing is free. Can you imagine that? The real essence of your life, that which you cannot stay without for two minutes, is free. It is free. But we do not appreciate these things. Free. The planet is free. Animals, birds, flowers, rivers are free. You go to the river and swim, and it is free. He is generous, but this generosity is related to our physical nature. We understand that. What about the mysteries that will reveal slowly the knowledge, the laws, the beauty which exist but we cannot see? All these things are generously given to us, if we are able to sit and enjoy them, to experience them, and to penetrate into them. Life is free. Of course, you pay the hospital to bring a child, but the child is free for you. God is so beautiful and generous.

To be generous means to have so much that you radiate it out. That is why generous people are like God. They give. They give.

The more you give, the more you receive; and the more you receive, the more you give. Then a day comes that you do not need to receive and to give because you are the gift. You really are. So be generous to be like Him, and slowly, slowly ponder and meditate upon the word "generosity."

What does it mean to be generous? The people who are not generous really are the losers because there is one great law: Whatever you give, you receive — exactly that. If you do not give, you do not receive. Generosity is the circulation of the energy that God has and the Universe has. Be generous.

The Watchful One

43

The Watchful One. If you call God the Watchful One, the One Who sees everything — your motives, your secret deeds or open deeds, your thoughts and emotions, your activities, your relationships, the letters you are writing, the gossip you are speaking, the slander you are spreading, the beautiful things which you have, the ugly things which you have — then you know that everything is watched. If we teach these things to our children and to ourselves, eventually we will come to our senses and realize that if someone is continuously, directly watching us, we really must behave.

When you see that the police are following you, you behave. When you know that your telephone is tapped, you know how to talk. If you start to think that He is the Watchful One, you will never do anything which will cause your conscience to bother you.

He is the Watchful One. In everything and everywhere He has His Eyes. A Great Teacher says, "God's Eyes are in every human being." That is very interesting. So He is a great spy! He is watching everything.

Then He says, "Your innermost Self is the Eye of God." Wow! The Monad that is within you, your innermost Self, is the Eye of God, and He watches you . . . through you. That is why no one can deceive himself, or herself. You are One with that Eye, and you are the Eye of that Great One, the Watchful One.

As you live a life of watchfulness, under the Watchful Eye of that great Power, you become a Watchful One. Your actions, your thoughts, your writings, your relationships with other people, your private life become so beautiful because every minute they are watched by you and by the Eye that is within you. When that Eye is within you, you cannot deceive yourself. The interesting thing is that sometimes we try to cheat and deceive others without realizing that *the same Eye is watching us through them.*

Many religions are created on this principle. They took this principle and turned it into a religion. Of course it is beautiful because they created the basic principles of how to live, how to relate to each other. But the principle is that the Eye within you is watching you and me just as my Eye is watching me and you. Then how can I dare to deceive you? That is why deception toward your brother is deception toward God.

Some people pray, "God, God, God, God." Then they kill others. How can they do that? Christ said something which is very beautiful. He said that you cannot love God unless you demonstrate that you love each other, that you love other human beings. See how the principles of religions are coming from the Ageless Wisdom.

People, nations, and groups cheat themselves. They say, "It is to our advantage to destroy them." It is not for their advantage. It is for their disaster because they are killing people in which the Eye of God is watching. If we understand these names of God, we have all the principles of how to live our lives.

The Responsive One
44

The Responsive One. Wow! This one is so beautiful. The Responsive One.

What is responsiveness? Great meditators, great initiates and Masters thought about God, "Who is God? What is God?" First they started asking, "What are all these stars, this or that?" and they found out that if these stars exist, if all these things exist, there must be a Cause behind them. Do you see? If my hands are moving, there must be somebody to move these hands.

So they started to search beyond. Who is that? What is that? The more they penetrated, the more they saw that it is the Infinite, but also that it *is responsive* everywhere and in everything.

What does it mean — responsive? It responds to your prayers, your wishes, your aspirations, your search. *Search and you will find it.* It is a response. *Knock and it will be opened. Ask and it will be given.* It is responsiveness.

Sometimes its response is very strange. There is a Sufi story which is so interesting. A man was hungry, so he went to his garden and started to pray,

"God, I am hungry. I am dying. Give me something to eat." Then suddenly a branch fell on his nose and hurt him. "My goodness, I was asking for dinner from You and You sent a dry branch to hit my nose. What am I going to do?" He ran to the river to wash his bloody nose. When he got there he saw that three big salmons were trapped in a little pool of water. "Ah," he said, "God, You did not give dinner to me but I found it."

God responded to the prayer by knocking him down, for who knows what reason, so that he goes and finds the salmon and cooks and eats them. The strange thing is that the man did not know it was an answer, a response to his prayer. So sometimes, if your prayers are answered or your aspirations are answered in some kind of painful way, accept it because there is a reason behind it!

All-Embracing One
45

All-Embracing One, All-Inclusive One. If this name is really pondered on and written about and broadcast through our radios and televisions instead of the usual criminal programs, you will see that people will slowly start to become inclusive, all-embracing.

There is a belief which is destroying humanity and it is called separatism. "Me and you. Ours and theirs. Ours is good and theirs is nothing. We are good; they are bad. We are saved; they are going to hell." But God is all-embracing. There is no this or that for God. When we understand that, eventually lots of irritation, anger, fights, and conflict will disappear because we will embrace everything that exists and heal it. That is the secret. Like a Mother embracing a little child who is wounded and comes crying to her, we will embrace everything and love it and heal it.

All human beings are going to develop that *name*, that principle. If you are not inclusive, you do not take part in the nature of God. You are outside! Only by being inclusive your value increases because you become a part of something great. But if you are separative, non-inclusive, you stay as you are and become rotten and die and disappear.

Everything that becomes inclusive grows and becomes more and more beautiful. So try to be inclusive. To be inclusive means that you do not harm anyone. You understand why they are like that, and you try to do your best to be inclusive . . . but not stupid. I must give this warning.

This really happened. A man in California was traveling with his wife and two children and they saw a man hitchhiking. The woman said, "You know, we must be inclusive. Let us take this man." They picked him up and the man pulled out a revolver and said, "Drive this way." Eventually he killed first the father and mother and then the children and disappeared.

Inclusiveness does not mean stupidity, naiveté. Inclusiveness means that principally you recognize each one's right to exist and you try to make each one's consciousness expand to such a degree that eventually you all create right human relations with each other. This is so important!

The Wise One

The Wise One. Isn't that something that you can call someone "wise"! Who is wise? The Wise One has tremendous experience. Imagine, God is experiencing everything that all human beings are experiencing. God is the hard disk in the computer. Every year the report comes there. He sees everything there. And He became so wise because wisdom is the ability to see the cause and effect simultaneously and to have the answer to change negativity into positivity, to make defeat a victory, to make loss a gain. That is wisdom — how to balance your life in such a way that you always are the winner, no matter if you lose, no matter if you fail.

In the physical plane you may fail, but in moral, intellectual, and spiritual planes you gain. Wisdom is to deal with life in such a way that always your progress is guaranteed. If you have wisdom, you are not trapped in anything. Neither sex, nor hatred, nor any limitation can trap you because wisdom makes you so intelligent that you know how to find your way toward your achievements, toward your spiritual destiny. That is what wisdom is.

God is wise. Why is He wise? It is because He knows everything that is happening, but in everything He slowly, slowly, through your defeat, through your failure, makes you eventually a victor. Do not forget that. It is called *Tactica Adversa* — how God brings beauty out of your ugliness, brings victory out of your failures and defeats, brings freedom out of your slavery. He Himself wants to be the Freed One, and He is the *You* within you.

The Loving One

47

The Loving One. Of course all religions, especially some who hate each other so much, speak about the Love of God. What is Love for me? Jumping over all the definitions of love in various writings, I like to speak about one thing through which I understand the deeper meaning of love. The love of God can be understood by the possibility and opportunity that He gave human beings to be perfect as "He is perfect." Do you understand how deep this is? If you love somebody, you want to make him greater and bigger and more majestic than you are. Humanity is given the opportunity to be like Him. That is love. He is the Loving One.

It is not emotional loving, it is not sexual loving, it is not conditional love; it is something which is given to everybody to develop and reach His perfection. Why is that? It is because love is the greatest magnet, and all of us are little, little iron pieces which are attracted to that Cosmic Magnet. That magnetism is His love which is pulling us slowly, slowly toward Him to be like Him. "Be perfect as your Father in heaven is perfect," said Christ. It is so beautiful.

The Gracious One
48

The Gracious One. This is fantastic. What does it mean to be gracious? Gracious means you, like a flower, are unfolding. The grace in you is blooming forth. That is you, the Chalice. If you see a little bud of a rose and it is growing and opening petal after petal, eventually you go to a friend and say, "How glorious this flower is." Why? — Because it is unfolded, because it has fragrance, because it has colors, and because it affects you, uplifts you, and opens your love toward it.

And we are going to be, each of us, gracious ones. For example, you come to a meeting. You feel that that lady is gracious or that man is gracious because he has unfolded the potentials that are within him. God's potentials that are within him are unfolding and expanding, releasing themselves. They are becoming so beautiful that the beauty surpasses our logic and reasoning and we say, "Wow," which means something that is beyond our comprehension, a glorious something. But in the human stage of consciousness, to be gracious means to unfold the Divinity that is within you and to live according to that unfolding Divinity. This means as you become gracious inside of you, you become gracious in your dressing, in your make-up, in your hairdo, in your speech, in your relationships, in your thinking. You are full of grace.

Can you imagine how many dirty thoughts we think daily? We curse and swear and do many, many ugly things, and then we want people to say we are gracious. It does not work. The grace, when unfolded within you, must appear outside in your relationships, in your manners, in your dressing, in your talking, in your expressions, in your writings, in everything you do. That is how you change from ugliness to grace.

Again we see, in repeating and thinking about the names of God we create an opportunity to be more than what we are now, and that is the progress of life.

The Resurrecting One
49

The Resurrecting One — He That resurrects you. This is very profound. You see, this is one level of interpretation of the names. One day, if we advance a little and we form specific groups and special classes, then we will go to the next dimension of interpretation of these names. What I am saying is not the whole thing. There are deeper and deeper layers in these names.

For example, the Resurrecting One means that eventually all of you are going to be resurrected, which means you are going to be the life itself. You are going to be conquering your physical, emotional, and mental vehicles. You are going to conquer death. And Who is doing all these things? All His Plans and Laws and Teachings and Wisdom are provided to us so that He resurrects us. Try to be resurrected ones, which means daily, yearly, try to break the limitations in which you are living — the limitations, the habits, the crystallized thinking, the automatic emotions, the physical crystallizations. Try to break these limits. Break these limits.

And if you break one of them every year, in sixty years you will be a resurrected one. Break your limitations, your laziness, your inertia.

The other day a girl called me and said, "I can't do meditation." I said, "Sit down and do meditation. Do it! Who is going to help you? You do it." Ten days later she called and said, "It is strange. After you said to do it, I am doing it." It was not because I said it but because she came to her senses. You can do it. You do not need a psychiatrist to take your hundred dollars for half an hour, psychoanalyze you, and say, "Your nose is too big. You cannot do meditation." You see? The Resurrecting One. It is so beautiful.

The Witness

The Witness. God is the Witness. Everything you are doing, good or bad, He is witnessing. Nothing is hidden and He witnesses you. If you lose something, if somebody steals from you, He is the Witness. You can cheat everybody except Him. If you are doing something great and nobody knows about it, God knows it. He is the Witness, and imagine how many good or bad things you did and He witnessed them.

Do you see how beautiful it is to discuss these names? He is the Witness. For millions of years you did things. He was the Witness there, just exactly there. Maybe you cheated everybody, but you cannot cheat Him. He is the Witness. He is the Witness of your achievement that even you cannot see. He is the Witness. He is seeing it.

Some scientists are trying in the eleventh hour to come to the surface and tell us that the whole Universe is a hologramic unit. Everything that is happening somewhere is happening everywhere, which means it is the Witness. He is That in everything. He is One.

Do not tell us that this is a new theory. We have known about it. Everything that is going on, He is the Witness. If we develop this sense, our progress will be Infinite and so beautiful, and all the things that we are wasting to kill people, butcher people, steal from people, impose certain rules and regulations upon people will eventually evaporate because we do not need anything like that. God is the Witness. It is so beautiful!

The Truth

51

He is *the Truth*. Wow! I had so much difficulty with this. What is the truth? Christ was beaten, and He wore that thorn crown. Pontius Pilate gave Him a slap on His face and said to Him, "Tell me, what is the truth?" and Christ looked into his eyes and kept silent. What was He going to say to him? You cannot understand truth when you are slapping the face of someone else. *Truth is the oneness, the one existence. There is no other Truth,* and everyone who is acting against oneness is acting against himself and committing suicide. That is the Truth. *Truth is Existence,* and no one *exists* except if he is *truthful.* Go think about it.

What does it mean, Truth means to exist? We do not really exist. We are here today, and tomorrow we are not. How are you going to exist?

Existence is achieved by the collective accumulation of the truths that you have expressed. If you are false, you do not exist. If you are a liar, you do not exist. If you are manipulative, you do not exist. If you are cheating people, you do not exist. You are a shadow. You will be evaporated very soon. Who exists? It is the one who is Truth.

The Trustee

The Trustee. God is called the *Trustee*. You trust Him. Your money is with Him. Your honor is with Him. Your future is with Him. Everything that you are, that you are going to be and have been is in His pocket, in His bank. He is the Trustee.

Sometimes we do good things and then say, "We did good things and they are lost. I gave two hundred dollars to that woman, but she never paid the money back. It is lost." If these things happen to you in your life, imagine that He is the Trustee. Somebody slandered you. God is the Trustee for your value, for your dignity, for your glory. He is the Trustee. He keeps your trust.

Do not be afraid at all when people are belittling and slandering you because your value, your dignity are entrusted to Him. They are there. Eventually you will find them, and they will make so much interest for you. Ten years later a slander will multiply into a glory for you. That is the secret when Christ said, "Bless them when they slander you." Why? Why am I going to bless them? They are putting a lot of money in your name with the Trustee. How nice.

King Akbar was said to have called his servant to ask, "Do you have a name of a new enemy?"

"Lord, why do you want a new enemy? We already have them."

"It is the enemies that make us greater."

Why do enemies make you great? — Because the Trustee keeps your honor, your dignity, your value in the bank. The increase of your enemies is a sign that you became more dangerous for them. The more you grow in power, the more enemies you attract . . . eventually to defeat them.

Because the Trustee protects your name and your work, He gives you more energy and power to defeat your enemies — who are also the enemies of the Trustee. Your relation with the Trustee becomes closer as your enemies attack you.

It is so bad, so dangerous to fight against the Trustee. Each time you gossip, slander, or belittle somebody, the Trustee notices it, and you will receive in due time whatever is necessary to send to you.

There is another Sufi story which is interesting. A boy went to a hotel and slept there. Another man entered the room and stole his wallet which contained two hundred dollars. The boy awoke and said, "My goodness, that is all that I had. Now I must go back home to get some money to continue my journey." He went home, and because he was very tired, he went to lay on his bed and felt something hard under the pillow. He looked at it and it was a wallet with five hundred dollars. "My goodness, I lost two hundred dollars, and here is five hundred dollars." Eventually the hotel called him. The man said, "We caught the man who stole your wallet, but unfortunately he had spent the money." The mother of the boy at home said, "We had a guest at night. He slept in your bed and the wallet you found is his wallet. He is the father of the man who stole your wallet." God is the trustee. If you lose here, do not worry. It is hidden there in the trust.

Q&A

Question: Two of the names are the Watchful One and the Witness. Could you distinguish between them?

Answer: Yes. The Watchful One is the One Who totally watches you but does not take action. It is a neutral watchfulness, like a man who is looking at you. He is not doing anything, but he scares you to death because he is looking.

The Witness is more about taking action. He knows what is happening. He records it. The Watchful One doesn't record but watches you. There is some difference.

Question: Are we affirming we are God when we say the mantram, "I am the Self?"

Answer: Of course, yes. You are pieces of God. You are sparks of the big fire.

We must realize that there is nothing else but God. We are pieces of God. We are sparks of the Living Fire. That is what we are going to realize.

When Christ said, "You are gods," they started to stone Him. Then He said, "In Psalm 82, David said, 'You are gods.' Why are you killing Me?"

This statement is in the Old and New Testaments, but these are echoes. What Christ said and the Old Testament said were recorded millions of years ago in the *Upanishads*, in the *Vishnupranas*, in the *Vedas*. What do the *Vedas* say? The One That is creating everything, everywhere is you. You are That; That is you. It is an old story, but knowing this does not matter at all. It doesn't help us. But if we actualize it and put it into our relationships, into our thinking, into our daily feelings, then it will make sense and develop the life and improve the life.

Before I continue with the fifty-third name of God, let me say a few words.

The problems of life — psychology, philosophy, science, business, taxes, politics, wars — have slowly filled our brains to the brim, and we do not have a place left for God. If we really think, we will see that maybe daily for one second we thought about God . . . or never. If we calculate the minutes we spoke about God, it would be maybe ten minutes a year. This means that our brain is filled with the trash that we have in our life. We need to empty that trash and fill our mind with some great energy, great vision, great idea because only in thinking about God and trying to be like Him can we progress on our Path and be happy, healthy, and prosperous.

Once Christ said, "Be perfect as your Father in heaven is perfect." Who is our Father and what is He? For example, we can say that He is the cause of everything that we see in the Universe. "From Whom everything proceeds, to Whom everything returns." Is there anything that did not come out of Him or will not go back to Him? By thinking about Him, we can see that He is the cause of all Cosmic and Universal Laws. Somebody, something must create these things.

Then we see that He is the Source of all energy. If there is any energy anywhere, He is in it. He *is* the energy. He is the Source of energy.

Then we see that all beauty is from Him. We can say also that He is the Source of beauty. If we think about beauty, slowly, slowly we can find a track going to Him. All beauty, all righteousness, all freedom eventually go and fuse with Him.

Then also we can say that He is the Source and Cause of all Light in any form. Whenever we see a candle, He is there. Whenever there is Light, He is there because He is the Light. He is the Love. Wherever there is Love, He is there. Then we can say that wherever there is Power, He is there because He is the Source of all Power. Then we can synthesize all these six things and say, "He is the cause of Life, the Source of Life, and we can add that He is Himself the Life." When you are living, that Life which is in you is Him. Sometimes in your retreat hours or when you are lonely or alone, you can think about Him.

When I went to some schools in the Far East, they gave me one hundred names of God. I asked, "What am I going to do with these?" They said, "By thinking about His names, you can slowly create some concept about Him because every name is one of His facets, one of His attributes."

So by thinking about His names, though He is nameless and we cannot measure Him with any name, we can measure Him by our concepts of what He may be. When we grow and expand our consciousness, either we see deeper meanings in His names, or we figure out a new name to name Him so that He becomes tangible for us. In thinking about His names, we slowly inject into our system His attributes. We like to be like Him because, actually, *none of us exists except Him.* That is such an important announcement and it is really the foundation of the future ages to come. We did not understand this. That is why we have so much trouble all over the world.

What is the foundation of the supreme civilization and culture that may come? The foundation is that *I am in you, you are in me, and we are all one in Him.* If we understand this, no problem exists. Even great, advanced Initiates or Masters tell us that when we are empty of God, we are full of problems and diseases. Do you understand this? It is so beautiful.

All misunderstanding and conflict, hatred, malice, all these things indicate one thing: that our mind, our soul is empty of Him. When He fills us, we exist as Him. We are closer to being like Him as we feel more of Him. The more He fills us, the more we become like Him. Isn't that beautiful?

Of course we ask, "Where is He?" The greatest proof that He exists is you. Look at your eyes and ears and mustaches and beards and organs and productivity and intelligence and creativity and this and that — these are you. But there is a secret there. If He is active in you, you are active in Him. If He is active in you, then He is controlling your mouth, your actions, your emotions, your ideas, your plans, your business. For example, if He is not in you, your business becomes monkey business. If He is in you, your business is His business. He made the business, and when He makes the business you become prosperous. That is the whole secret. When nations are becoming poor and starving, you will see one thing. They were very busy with their own business, and God never did business through them. You build a car and one year later you cry, "The car is not selling." Why? It is because you put trash into that car. Do you see that? It is so practical. It did not satisfy the customers.

So, speaking and thinking about God approximates our psychology, our philosophy, our beingness, our whole attitude toward Him. Eventually we reach a point where we become so cautious that we do not do anything without asking Him. Did you ever ask Him? Those who ask Him, they know the right thing to do. For example, one day I was talking with a drug seller. I asked, "Before you sold these drugs, did you ask God?" "You are crazy," he said. Eventually he was shot and put into prison. When I visited him I asked, "How do you feel?" "Well, I am all right." "Did you know that if you had asked God before you sold drugs, you would not be here?" "Well," he said, "I figured it out."

It is so easy to say these things, but eventually we come to our senses. It is a very painful process. We come to our senses; we swallow our vanity, ego, and pride; and then before we do anything, we create a communication line with Him and ask Him, "Do you think this plan is all right?" If you feel in your heart that He said it is all right, it is all right. I am not talking about mediumship, channeling, psychic phenomena. It is God and you, with nothing in between.

Let us see the rest of the names of God.

The Strong One

53

The Strong One. His name is the Strong One, the Strength. Can you imagine anything stronger than the Cause of this whole Universe? In the 1970 earthquake in California, two or three commentators on television and radio, who had never believed in God, said, "He shakes a little and everything is ruined. What a power that is." One of them said, "I feel so humiliated that we do not have strength." You do not. Where is your strength?

I had a friend who was a boxer. One day he fainted. As we took him to the hospital, his hands and feet were trembling. He asked me, "Where is my strength?" I said, "Your strength is gone because you did not ask the Strong One how to use your strength. Killing, beating others and bringing blood from their nose and ears, is that a nice thing to do with your strength?"

So here we can learn something. God is the Strength. He is the Strength. Wherever there is strength, He is there. He is in your muscles. He is in your nervous system. He is in your aspiration, dedication, work, striving. He is the strength of your courage and daring. If you see something that is strong, remember that is Him. In this way you can worship Him everywhere there is strength. Strength is so beautiful. I remember an old man who said, "I wish I were twenty-four or thirty. My strength is gone." That is true. It is so beautiful to have strength.

Remember these names and sometimes sit and meditate on what is the strength. Do you really have the Source of strength? You do not. That is the amazing thing. It is given from somewhere else to you. It is in the sun. It is in the planet. It is in the food. It is given to you. When it is taken, you are an empty bag which collapses.

Strength is also in your emotions. For example, when I went to Italy to the monastery of Saint Francis of Assisi, I was amazed at the strength of the man who built that monastery. The walls were maybe two hundred feet high. From the abyss to the top, the monastery and walls were built by his own hands. What kind of strength is this, and who gave it to him? This strength was given to him by the vision he had about God. That strength is there. If you have a vision, you have strength because every right vision is Him. It is Him! Do you see how beautiful it is? So think about strength.

The Firm One
54

The Firm One. When you are building a cathedral or a big building, you want one thing. You want the foundation to be firm. If you are driving, you do not want the freeway to go zigzag. You want it firm. If you are making an agreement, you want it firm. If you love somebody, it must be firm.

Do you know how many people love and there is no firmness in it? You can see something secret there. Wherever there is no firmness, there is no love, there is no friendship, there is no agreement, there is no understanding. There is no cooperation if firmness is lacking. How can you build a building upon a foundation that always shakes? You cannot.

Every great thing that you are going to build must have firmness in it. Your speech must be firm — not yes and no, maybe, perhaps. That isn't firm.

People are so intelligent. They say the words *almost, perhaps, maybe, I guess so, they said so.* There is no firmness in those words. Yes, or no! That is why Christ said, "Your yes will be *yes,* and your no will be *no.*" There is no fluctuation. If you say, "I love you," okay, show it. Firmness.

In everything that you see in the world that is firm, you can feel His Presence in the firmness. Instinctively you hate anything that has no firmness. Right? Think about it. You are engaged to a woman or a man, but there is no firmness. Until it is firm, you feel "icky" and you do not digest your food. Really! For example, when you go fishing on a choppy ocean, the boat bobs up and down. What happens to your stomach? You become sick. Why? There was no firmness. Until you are firmly in God, you are sick.

Your faith will be firm. Your understanding must be firm. Your friendship must be firm. When you shake a person's hand, you know whether that man or woman is firm or not firm.

What happens if you develop strength — physical strength, psychological strength, spiritual strength, divine strength? If you become firmer in your physical, emotional, mental, and spiritual relationships, what happens? You become a little closer to Him. A little part of your soul is filled with Him, and then what happens? You transcend your stupidities and vanities and become more human. That is it!

Whoever says that thinking and talking about the hundred names of God is not practical is absolutely wrong. It is really practical because it changes your whole life. Are you firm in your friendship, are you firm in your promises, or do you change every minute?

I was talking to a boy who everyday had a new girlfriend. I said, "When are you going to be firm?" "What do you mean?" he said. These ideas are not there, but violence, murder, and wars are there. Our children are seeing them morning and night, but they are never taught about being firm. Firmness is absolute dedication, absolute devotion to something glorious.

The Protecting Friend

55

The Protecting Friend. In Sufism they call God "the Protecting Friend." If you have any friend which you can really, really believe in, that is Him. Your friends will leave you. Maybe your husband, your wife, your children, even, will forget about you. But there is One Who never leaves you. That is Him.

Why can He not leave you? — Because you are Him. How can you leave yourself? Do you see how beautiful it is?

Whenever any friends, anybody around you, beyond you, behind you, above you deserts you, you must know there is One Who is really the Protecting Friend. Everybody, everything which you have faith in may deceive you, but one thing will never deceive you! It is Him.

Isn't it nice psychologically to have such a vision, such a thought that there is at least somebody who never betrays you? One day a woman was crying and crying. I asked, "What happened?" "My husband is going with other girls." "I would never have imagined that," I said, "but Somebody did not leave you." "Who? Everybody I went with left me." I said, "Do you know that God never left you? Think about it."

It is so beautiful to have the psychological attitude in life that there is Someone you can really have faith in, and that He is going to stand there no matter who or what you are and protect you. Christ gave this example in a very beautiful way. What did He say? "There was a very rich man with two children. One of the children said, 'Daddy, give me everything which belongs to me and I will go.' He took all his money and belongings and left. He became so poor and degenerated. Eventually one day He thought, 'Am I stupid? My Father has palaces and everything, and I could live there like a king. Why am I staying here? Let me go back,' meanwhile thinking that Daddy will not look at his face. Just the opposite happened. His Daddy said, 'My son, you are welcome.'" Look at what a beautiful feeling that is! When you have made many errors in your life, many mistakes in your life, when there were many things which you did wrong, no matter how muddy or polluted you were, do not worry. You have a Friend.

One day I was saying to myself, "You know, I do not like you anymore," and Torkom asked, "Why not?" I said, "I do not like you." Then I felt so lonely. I asked, "Who is going to like me? Of course, there are many who are ready to like me." But I asked, "Who is the firm One Who will like me?" Immediately I thought about God, and every anxiety vanished. What is this? This is psychotherapy. This is healing.

A psychiatrist once said to me, "You know, what you are talking about is not reality." Why is it not reality if it is healing, if it is taking me from depression and making me happy, healthy, and prosperous? What is better than that? It is not pills and injections.

One hundred names of God. . . . Each of them is a panacea for health, happiness, prosperity, and success.

The Praiseworthy One

56

The Praiseworthy One. When you see an artist draw something, you say, "You are a very beautiful artist. You are perfect." You see another girl singing and you say, "Wow! I applaud you. I express my gratitude to you." You praise him or her. If your little boy or little girl did something beautiful, what do you say? "I love you. I praise you." You may even give some gifts.

Is there anyone more praiseworthy than Him? Go at midnight and look at the stars. You will "flip out." Why are you not thinking about Him? Why are you not giving praise to Him? Giving praise to Him can be a lip service. But if you really understand and feel that He is praiseworthy, you uplift your consciousness and recognize Him and feel gratitude for all that you are enjoying. When you feel that gratitude, you come one inch closer to Him . . . and that is the miracle. You come one inch closer just by thinking about Him.

Now you can say, "We know now that we have *strength,* we have *firmness, friendship, trustworthy friendship, a protector,* and *praiseworthiness.* Do you see how the names are linking together? When you link all these together, you have a little idea about Whom you are thinking even though it is impossible to put in the cup of our brain the Universe.

There is a story about two little children who said, "Let's empty this ocean." Then they thought, "How can we empty it?" They took a nut and broke it into two halves to make two nutshells. One said, "I will hold this half and you bring the water from the ocean and pour it into my shell. Eventually we will finish it." There was a scientist sitting nearby thinking about the Universe, about God, about Creation, and so on. He saw that the children were so busy emptying the ocean. He went to them and said, "What are you doing?" They said, "We are trying to empty the ocean so that we can walk there." "Are you crazy?" the scientist asked. "That is not possible." Then one of the boys, or some angel around there, said, "Then how can you empty the mystery of Creation, of manifestation into your little, stupid brain?"

Of course, everyone knows everything! A politician can solve all problems in one second if you vote for him. A doctor can heal everything but cannot heal his hatred, his greed, his jealousy, his revenge. I was talking to a doctor who had just graduated from school. I asked, "What are you going to heal now?" "Now that I am in business, I will heal everything." "Well, you divorced your wife yesterday. Why didn't you heal that?" "What are you talking about? That is not healing," he answered. "Really?" Then one month later he called me and said, "I have a very, very bad headache." "It is because you divorced your wife," I replied. "Heal yourself."

This is it. If you think that you are almighty, that you can do everything and anything, wait a minute and think that there is some great mystery that you cannot put into your mind and you are only a little cell in the Universe, nothing else. A statement by the Great Sage impressed me so deeply. He said that we are like "dry leaves scattered in the Universe." There is only one firm anchorage. It is the Hierarchy. Firmness. It is God that is active in Them. Now that was Praiseworthiness

The Accountant

The Accountant. All your monkey business He knows! God knows your physical, emotional, and mental business. He knows! His nose is in everything, so do not change your books. He is the accountant of your speech, of your thoughts, of your feelings, of your secret, mysterious transactions. He has the accounting business. He has the Karmic Lords. In the hard disk of God's computer, your accounting is there. If you cheated, the accounting is there. It is awful, isn't it? It is awful, but that is the way it is. It is better to know about this than to fool around and cheat and deceive people. How intelligent the Sufis were to figure out that God must have a name and that name must be the Accountant.

Be careful with your accounting because He is there and He is looking. What great changes will happen in our psychology and business and life, in the White House, in the Senate, in Congress, in great, great businesses! What a change will happen in the world if suddenly we realize that the Accountant is going to research. God does not even need to research. He knows what is going on. An IRS man told me that he went to a church and they had two accounting books, one for the IRS and one for the Bishop. It was different accounting. But if you know that the Accountant is there and looking at the books, you will be a little careful what you are going to put in the books.

It is not only for business. We must not belittle the idea and say that what we are talking about is for business. It is not. We are talking about your "thought" accounting. I received a letter from a leader. He said, "I am writing this letter to apologize to you. I cursed you a hundred times. I hated you. I was so jealous of you." I never expected this letter, and when he came here from a faraway state, he hugged me and said, "You are my vision."

I do not care if he hates or loves me. So what! But, we are going to give an accounting of what we did physically, emotionally, mentally, and spiritually in our service, in our relationships. Everything is recorded in the ledger. The Karmic Lords have a complete recording. They feel and know everything. Everything is accounted for.

The Originator

58

The Originator. This is so beautiful. Is there anything glorious that has not originated from Him — all the races, all the vegetation, all the fish. But we are killing them every day with our pollution. Imagine all the birds whose lungs we are poisoning. They cannot breathe anymore.

Years ago I wrote *The Unusual Court,* but only a few of you have read it. Shame on you! Buy that book and read it. It is about the philosophy of pollution and destruction and how we can get rid of it. It is in that little book.

Originator. Every Goodness, Beauty, Righteousness, Joy, Freedom, striving toward perfection, and sacrificial service originated from Him. The Great Master says that the roses we see are so beautiful with their radiant color and perfume, but if we could just see and smell the astral roses and mental roses! Their perfume goes for miles. The Great Sage tells us that our good thoughts rise in space and suddenly pop out like a flower in the presence of Christ: "A pure thought ever ascends. At the feet of

Christ it blossoms, radiant...."[1] Do you see how beautiful it is? Think about the Originator.

All that exists originated from Him. We must cultivate gratitude and admiration for every leaf and Galaxy that He originated.

---

1. Agni Yoga Society, *Leaves of Morya's Garden* I, para. 21.

The Provider

The Provider. This is very interesting. I was thinking about what He has provided. Look at what a list: water, soil, air, sunshine, energy, intellect, consciousness. What else do you want? It is all free. It is not even taxed. What will happen if He does not give sunshine? Provider. But this is only the physical. He is also the provider of those graceful, subtle, magnificent emotions, feelings; that complicated, most beautiful, mysterious thinking, ideas, revelations, impressions, inspirations; that great plan that you have and purpose that you have; that contact you have. Look how much is provided.

You can sit and create a computer, for example. You can sell the computer, but the Originator does not take any money for it. He gave it to you. Right? It is an interesting point to think about. The Originator is not interested in taking anything from you when He is giving. What is the secret? *It is because He is giving to nobody. He is giving to Himself.* How can one make business with himself? He is giving the sunshine to Himself, to His babies, children,

Sparks. But look how much monkey business we do with things He gave to us for free.

The Quickener

60

The Quickener. What does it mean — The Quickener? The Quickener means, psychologically, esoterically, the One Who inflames you, kindles you, gives you enthusiasm, devotion, fire, steam. Look at how nice this is! You open a business, and you do not sit there like a donkey. You work. You do something. From where did that energy come? That energy came from Him. He is the Quickener. He quickens your physical body, emotional body, mental body, and then you say, "Early every morning at five o'clock I must get up and do my business — not sleep until ten." Then you say, "There is a friend who needs me. I must go and help him." That is the Quickener. Something is quickened within you.

When you feel quickening experiences, you immediately must think it is coming from Him. It is not even coming from Him. He is visiting you. A depressed man or a depressed woman is not visited by Him. If you gave up and are only thinking about suicide, the Visitor has departed from you. That is what is happening. It is not this chemical, that chemical going out of your brain. It is because He left you, taking all the chemicals with Him. That is why you are depressed. If He is within you, He is the Quickener. You are dead tired, but suddenly the phone rings and a friend says, "I had an accident. Please help me." "Okay," and you jump. That is the Quickener. That is your Soul, the Divinity within you that is quickening you.

The Destroyer

The Destroyer. Ah, this one is so beautiful. God is called the Destroyer. Have you seen hurricanes? Have you been in an earthquake? Have you heard of submerged continents? When things become obstacles to the progress of human beings, He destroys them so that He paves the way for you to contact Him.

He is the destroyer of what? — Of anything that is false, of everything that is a barrier to your progress, of everything that will bring you pain and suffering and destruction. He wipes them out . . . if you let Him do it.

The Destroyer. He is the destroyer of your bad thoughtforms and emotions and habits. The other day I experienced this very beautifully. A boy called and said, "I decided to go to my girlfriend's home and beat her." I said, "Do not make that thoughtform because you will do it if you build it strongly enough." "Well, that is what I am going to do." I said, "Think about God. Think about the Master." I gave him some things to think about. He called me back and said, "Why did you say those things to me?" I asked, "What is the matter?" "I cannot go now and beat her."

One minute of elevating your consciousness, of transforming your consciousness destroys your bad thoughtforms, your bad feelings, your bad plans, even your habits and bad motives.

Later, maybe you and other people will sit down and take these names of God and formulate into lessons this practical discipline, how to do these things. That is what we were doing in the schools. It must be scientifically formulated with illustrations and color. That is what I did in the past. I remember thinking, "Destroyer? I hate destruction!" But then I started to love the name so much. Wow! If we destroyed these habits of drug use, alcoholism, if we destroyed these thoughtforms of hatred, of wars, and different things, what else could we want? That is why the Great Master, talking about Shamballa energy, which is one of the attributes of God, says that It is the broom of God. It washes away things from higher planes to lower to pave the way for progress.

We also read in Hindu writings that Shiva — one of their Gods — is the Destroyer.

When we say "hundred names of God," people sometimes think, "How come God has one hundred names?" All these names are the attributes, the various sides of the diamond. It is one diamond, but there are many, many facets of the diamond. Also, each name is the diamond, and the diamond is all the names. But why have these hundred names? In ancient Teachings the great Rishis and great wise people say that we must always think, feel, live, and act in the Presence of God.

There are some practices in the Middle East and Far East in which you always repeat the names of God. Whatever name you remember you can repeat, or you can repeat hundreds of them. Actually they have a string of a hundred beads, and they start naming the first name, second name, third name, fourth name, and so on, counting on the beads.

This exercise is not given to become mechanical in repeating the names and forgetting about them. There is a great secret in it. Every time you repeat a name, you are sounding one of the notes of the Cosmic Symphony. The Symphony — the notes within you — is becoming orchestrated and complete. When you repeat the names with attention and with an effort to impress upon your mind the qualification of the name, then you are bringing that Symphony within your consciousness, within your psyche, and you are resounding to the music that is in the spheres.

Some people think that it is a mechanical process to repeat the names of God, but it is not mechanical. You can, of course, make it mechanical by thinking about something else while making your mouth repeat the names. That does not help. Actually it helps a little because the vibration, the sound around you, creates some purification.

Science is beginning to understand that everything is vibration, radiation. Even when you mechanically repeat the names, you are creating in your etheric body, astral body, and mental body a specific vibration which is tuning, orchestrating, integrating your aura and building a powerful radioactivity which is repelling many physical, emotional, mental, and spiritual attacks on you. That is what the names are for. But instead of repeating the names mechanically, we can repeat them with understanding, impressing our inner consciousness, and slowly, slowly start a process of transmutation in our system.

All day we are flooded, contaminated with various energies and forces. Of course, in space there are millions of crisscrossing good and bad, positive and negative energies which contaminate us, but the most contaminating sources are human beings with their ugly thoughts, their destructive thoughts, their negative emotions, hatred, revenge, jealousy, with their very ugly physical vibrations, and also with their vibrations of sickness. Even sickness radiates. If you have a certain kind of sickness, you radiate it and contaminate space.

Repeating these names brings a cleansing in your aura and strengthens you. Eventually your aura, your vibration, your electromagnetic sphere becomes so powerful that the pollution coming from outside does not contaminate you anymore.

There is another side of contamination. You are not only a target of outer contamination. You understand outer contamination. When you think about somebody evilly, negatively, when you slander mentally or send waves of hatred and jealousy, these kinds of things, you contaminate people. These are outside things. There is also inside contamination.

The first source of inside contamination is your subconscious. There is a lot of trash in your subconscious and sometimes this contamination comes to your waking consciousness and impresses itself to such a degree that you think that you are the one thinking these naughty, stupid thoughts. That is an inner attack.

Also, your imaginations become sources of your attacks. For example, fifty days ago you were imagining something ugly. Now, when it is restimulated by chance or for some reason, that imagination immediately gets into your consciousness and forces you to act according to your imagination. These are inner attacks. When you are voicing the names of God, you repel those inner and outer forces.

A lot of Hindus and Far Eastern people believe that one of the greatest names of God is AUM. It is so powerful that by repeating it slowly, slowly you annihilate attacks coming to you from inside and outside.

We could talk about this for a long time but let's come to the subject. We are now on sixty-two!

First, understand the meaning. Later, if you want to do it, you can go home and repeat the names or, better, make them seed thoughts for your meditation.

The Ever-Living

The Ever-Living. One day I asked my Teacher what Ever-Living meant. He said, "There is no end or beginning for Him. He lives always." He lives throughout Nature. He lives in every form. He lives in space. He lives in matter. He is the One Who lives, and every life is an expression of this livingness. It is so beautiful.

Sometimes you think that you are living, actually, in reality, He is living through you. He is the living One within you.

Another day I asked my Teacher, "What is the Ever-Living One?" He said, "Come, come," and he took me to his office where he showed me a big bouquet of evergreen flowers. Do you know that violet flower that never fades? They were so beautiful. He said, "Remember, we collected these flowers ten years ago. Still they have the same color, the same beauty. This is a very, very small example for you of ever-livingness. Now," he said, "He is Ever-Living, but when you unite and fuse your consciousness with Him, you will be Ever-Living."

We die, we come back, we die, we come back, we die, we come back, but we never remember what happened in the past or what is going to happen in the future. The Ever-Living is the always conscious One. In all changes He is living. We are going to be the Ever-Living One by building our consciousness thread and always being conscious in our death and birth — how we are going to take birth, how we are going to die but without losing our consciousness. That is Ever-Livingness. Try to be this ever-living for yourself. Identify with that idea, with that vision. It is so important.

Ideas are energies. When you identify with energies, transmutation and transformation take place within your nature. Ideas, Ever-Livingness, God, Ever-Living, . . . Ever-living. In every living form, in every living being, He is the living One.

The Self-Existing One

The Self-Existing One. No one created Him. He existed. The name is so beautiful. It is even beyond our comprehension. Self-Existing.

Everything that exists in this world is caused by something. It has a source, but the idea here is that He is sourceless. He is the cause. He is not an effect. We are effects. Mother, Daddy came together, and we are here. Mother and Daddy are the source, but He has no source. It is so beautiful to transcend the limits of our reasoning and logic and totally reverse ourselves, introducing the idea into our mind that there are causeless things, self-existing things. No one created them, no one shaped them, no one characterized them, but they are absolute Be-ingness. Think about it.

Does it help to think about this concept? Of course, yes. In your essential essence you are the Self-Existing One. The trick is that this Teaching is going to bring a revelation into your mind so that you stop being a result of things — the result of your emotions, the result of your judgment and criticism, the result of your wishes and desires, the result of your bodies. You exist because you think you are a body. Isn't that pitiful?

Every one of us thinks we exist because we have our body. If the body is taken away, we think that it is a catastrophe. Everything is finished. What this concept of God is introducing is totally different. You are the Self-Existing One, and you are really the source which gives existence to your body, to everything that you have. It is so beautiful to know that you are the Self-Existing One. Dwell on that thought.

You are not a result. Listen to this very carefully. It is very subtle. You are not going to join your bodies and tell yourself that you are the result of these bodies, that you are not self-existent. That is where you are losing. The greatest sin you can commit is thinking that you are not the Self-Existing One. Look how it will lift you suddenly from the sewage of life to the light of the sky. You are the Self-Existing One. And because you now know that One, there is a tremendous responsibility within you to live as a Self-Existing One and not to live as a slave of your bodies, of your emotions, of your thoughts and judgments and criticisms and feelings because then you are becoming a result. It is so beautiful.

Self-Existing One. Nothing exists beyond Him, before Him, after Him. He is the Self-Existing One. This name also helps us to break the crystallization of the time concept in our mind. We are always related to the time concept — today, tomorrow, one hundred days, four hundred days, one hundred years. This is a human creation. Our minds created such concepts, and, because we created them, we became the slaves of these concepts. Here, just the opposite is happening. Great Beings are giving some ideas through which we are enabled to break the time concept and think about the timelessness of human existence. Did you see that? It is a great release for us.

The Noble One

The Noble One. God is called the Noble One. The meaning of nobility is very, very strange. People think that because you are coming from kings and queens you are a noble. This idea was prevalent from the 14th century to the 18th century. Eventually people destroyed the idea of nobility. Even if you talk about nobility, people think you are talking about capitalism or about dictatorship, totalitarianism, this or that.

But what is nobility? Nobility is nothing else but a realization of God within you. That is nobility. It is so easy to understand. When you reach the God-realization within you and you think that you are the Self-Existing One, you are One with Him. How beautiful. Then you start becoming noble.

What does it mean to be noble? To be noble means that in your thoughts, in your emotions, in your relationships, you demonstrate power, beauty, love, freedom, direction, and purity. When these are demonstrated through you, you are becoming a noble person. You cannot be a noble person if you are the slave of your cheating, deceptions, hatred, jealousy, revenge, fear, separatism, fanaticism, or greed. Then you cannot be noble. It is impossible.

Nobility starts when the God within you begins to express Itself through all your actions. That is why Buddha sometimes said in His Teachings, "My Noble Ones." He called His Arhats, "The Nobles." Why? An Arhat is a man who has just started to contact the God within him. Arhats are just in the beginning of self-actualization, self-realization, so Buddha called them, "My Noble Ones." Noble Ones are those whom you trust. You trust your love to them. You trust your money, your honor, your beauty, your name to them. You trust them. They are nobles. This is so beautiful.

I composed some music which is called "The Dance of Nobles." You must hear it one day. It is so beautiful. That is self-praise. But that is not me, you see. It is Him, Him within me.

Always I realize when I start to write something good, when I do something good, when I help somebody — one second a thought comes in my mind, "Torkom, you did it," but I say, "Stop it. It's not you. It's not you. It's Him." Then you disappear, and He exists within you. That is how you can reach, slowly, slowly, to nobility — availing yourself and opening the gates for the King within you.

The Glorious One

The Glorious One. What is glory? Glory is something beyond your reason and logic, beyond your principles and standards. It is beyond.

I noticed when I went to great mountains and rivers and lakes and saw tremendous beauty and rainbows and aureolas something surprising happened within me. Suddenly, in that beauty something shut off in me. The lower man stayed there, and something opened that was not logic, was not reasoning. It did not respond to logic and reasoning, mathematics, geometry, etc. It was something beyond. You enter the Intuitional Plane and grasp it, but you do not have any ways or means to translate it. That is the glory. You don't have thoughts yet. You don't have emotions yet.

I remember one thing that happened, and I noted it in my diary that day. It was so beautiful. We were ten boys climbing a mountain in the early morning to greet the sun. Suddenly it came to us to sleep on the side of the mountain and reach the summit in the early morning before the sunrise. We slept well and, early morning, awakened. The sun was not yet there. When the sun started to come through the clouds in that wilderness of mountain ranges, the boys started to jump and dance.

I said, "Why are they doing that?" and I started to cry. It was so beautiful that one could not do anything. Feeling was too much. Reasoning was impossible because it was beyond feeling and reasoning. So, what happened? My whole body was hot, I was perspiring in that early morning, and I was crying, but the boys were dancing. I thought maybe dancing had a profound significance because through our movements we say things to Nature or to people that otherwise we never could do.

Then I started slowly to understand how the animals talk to each other. They wag their tail back and forth, and it means ten sentences. It is so different. Then sometimes you perceive or notice how people look or give a little wink and so on. If you translate this, it is half a page but it took one second. It is the Glorious One within you, and the Glorious One is Something that when He starts to manifest through you you will never find any words to formulate what it is. What is it that is making you to wonder? The glory in you is touching the glory in others, and it is making the life glorious — something which is beyond your level.

If you do not have that sense of glory, you are living like the gophers under the ground. You catch a little gopher and you tell him, "There are eagles." He will laugh at you and say, "What are you talking about?" Because he cannot believe in the existence of eagles, he remains always a gopher.

What about us? We must transcend ourselves. How beautiful it is even sometimes to look at yourself and say, "You know, I really don't know this man. Who is he?" That means you have made a quantum jump into the Infinite Domain. One minute is enough to destroy all your crystallizations.

How do these things happen? They happen by thinking about concepts like these we are giving. It is a great opportunity to talk about glory, to talk about nobility. It is an opportunity for you to rub your soul with these high concepts and become electrified with them — or else you are living the gopher life.

The Unique One

66

The Unique One. Unique. *The Unique One* gives me the feeling that there is no comparison with it. Can you compare God with anything? It is impossible. He is Unique. If you sit and say, "The Unique One," and think a little, "The Unique One," suddenly you realize that there is something happening within your nature also. What is it? You suddenly realize that in your essence you are really unique. You are **really** unique! Every human being is so unique, and that is why human beings are so precious.

Of course we can have tensions, we have emotions, thoughts, but finally we realize that everyone is unique *who is not identified* with his body, emotions, and mind . . . because then he is not unique. He is common. What this name is essentially saying is, "Every one of you must try and strive to be unique. In your beauty you are going to be unique. In your speech you are going to be unique. In your creativity you are going to be unique."

What does it mean to be unique? It means you are not common anymore. You are not part of the cattle. You are unique now. You are somebody and something. Why are you somebody and something? It is because the Unique One within you began to manifest through you. You are not going to be unique for the sake of uniqueness and for the sake of self-esteem or self-praise. You are going to be unique because you are manifesting the Unique One through yourself. The more unique you become, the more you become Him.

The uniqueness of man is expressed when he blooms from his own seed, his own individual potentials, without making himself common or pretending to be like others or like movie stars. Real uniqueness is in the uniqueness of his consciousness, his viewpoints, his ideas, his values.

The One

67

The One. In all numbers, in all geometry, without the number one there is nothing. He is the beginning and end. He is the One.

What does it mean to be One? To be One means that you are a tree and you have billions of branches and flowers and leaves, but you are the one tree. Humanity, when it understands this concept, will come to the conclusion that every human being, every animal, every tree, every bush, and every flower are just like bulbs through which one electricity manifests. This concept, of course, will save all these slaughters, wars, taxes, destructions, hatreds, and tensions because then we will see that the One is living in every form, as one electricity in billions of bulbs. If you shut off the electricity, all the bulbs go out. That is the One.

Actually, it is the same within our body, you see. What is the life of this finger? Me. What is the life of my toe? Me. When I leave this body, the life is gone. It is the One. Think about it. It is the One.

In the Bible and in every true religion they say that there is Only One, nothing else. If you start worshiping other things, you are on the wrong path. You must worship only the One in everything — the One.

If you think of worshiping this and worshiping that as separate forms, you are actually not worshiping. You can worship *only* the One, worshiping everything for the One . . . the One.

We can find something very beautiful in the Upanishads. I never found any other place with such a philosophy, such a beautiful metaphysics. It says, "We love our friends, we love our wives and husbands, we love our co-workers not because we love them but because we love the One within them." Here, if you are hating anyone, you are hating the One Who is in everyone. That is the real religion. That is the real philosophy. If you are based in separatism physically, emotionally, mentally; if you are worshiping your separate existence, your group existence, your national existence, you are really on the wrong side. You are destroying that Oneness which is trying to manifest Itself through the One that is within you. Think about it.

The Absolute

The Absolute. This is *the Eternal Support of Creation, the Source of Everything*. This word reminds me of ideas which Buddhists or esotericists use. They speak about voids, emptiness or they speak about space, free of imperfections, limitations, restrictions, and conditions.

Actually, the Absolute is in every human being, in every atom or form. The deeper you go into the *microcosmic* form, the more you meet the Absolute. The deeper you go into the *macrocosm*, the more you meet the Absolute.

I found that meditating on the word "Absolute" gradually annihilates all limiting thoughts from your mind, all separatism, all criticism, even all judgment.

When during the meditation you penetrate into the formless world, the Light of the Absolute slowly penetrates into your mind and the revelation of the Absolute becomes slowly possible.

Meditation on the Absolute fills your heart with bliss, patience, and divine indifference. The appearance of objects, forms, animals, birds, and human beings ceases to be the limit of what they are. Their appearance stands as an open door to penetrate beyond.

Those who meditate on the Absolute find themselves above their worries, anxieties, and irritations. One gets closer to the Absolute by thinking about the Absolute.

My experience is that such a kind of meditation must not take more than five minutes, and during days of such meditation the person must engage himself in objective labor to keep himself grounded.

The Able One

The Able One. This one is very important, very beautiful. All the "ability" that you have is from Him. It comes from your soul and your soul is one little, little leaf in Him. The Able One.

How can we see that He is the Able One? Go at midnight and watch the stars, or watch yourself in the mirror and see how you were created. What a masterpiece you are! You are a masterpiece — your hair, your eyes, everything. You are a masterpiece. Your heart is a masterpiece. Your hearing, your seeing is a masterpiece. The Able One can create something like that. What about the planets, Galaxies, Solar Systems, Zodiacs, millions of Zodiacs? You think there is only one Zodiac. There are millions of them. Behind the black holes, there is another Universe there. The Able One.

If He is the Able One, what do we learn from this? Christ said, "Be perfect as My Father in Heaven is perfect." You are going to be an able one. When we say, for example, "Mr. this or Mrs. that is able," what did he or she do? The able one created a great business or built a university of wisdom. The able one created books, paintings. He is becoming an Able One. He is not "tomatoes," "potatoes." He became an able one, an efficient one.

Most of our little ones and teenagers do not have these concepts. We are going to inspire and tell them, "Be able." Develop abilities — physical, emotional, mental, technical, spiritual, Divine abilities — so that eventually in every step of your life you demonstrate a new dimension of ableness. That is why the Great Sage gave the Shamballa prayer: *O Thou Who called me to the path of labor, accept my ableness* .... What does it mean "accept my ableness"? It means that because of my ability, because I am becoming able like You, I have the right now to expect that You will accept me. I am not sitting here and begging for money and stealing money or killing people for their money. I am able. I can create.

It is a shame that we have all over the world millions of unemployed people. What a shame is this! Where is this idea? There are lots of opportunities everywhere. You can create money from the stones if the spirit is given to you that you are able. Ableness. That is so beautiful.

There is another idea that is tied to ableness. What is this idea? *Nothing is impossible.* Nothing is impossible. Everyone who has really made breakthroughs in any field of human endeavor is an *able* one. What does it mean to be an able one? An able one is a person who has refused to accept the idea of impossibility. You can write a book about this.

At one time I had fifty cents in my pocket. I was going to California and somebody asked me,

"Why are you going to California? Work in my factory."

I said, "What am I going to do in your factory?"

"You are going to make purses for the ladies."

I told him, "No, I am going."

"What are you going to do?" the man asked.

Until today I remember his laugh when I told him, "I will write books and people will read them!"

I put my hand immediately into my pocket and found my beads. I said to myself, "The Able One, the Able One, the Able One, the Able One, the Able One," and told the man, "You are crazy, stupid."

"Who told you?" the man asked.

"My beads! My beads told me that you are really stupid."

"Why?"

"Because You are making me believe I cannot do it."

You make people believe they are no good, they are weak, they are stupid, they have failed, they are defeated, they are rascals. You are going to make each other able.

Do not say, "Yuck. Is that all you can do? I knew that. You were always like that — a potato." What are you doing? You are not doing something very small. You are attacking the Able One within the person. You are attacking the God Who is sitting within him with your stupidity, making that God believe that he is nothing, he cannot do it, he cannot be successful, he cannot achieve, he cannot understand. You say, "Who are you to understand that book? You are a cabbage."

We hear this from our fathers, mothers, friends that we are stupid. That is why we have created cattle in the world. And who are these cattle? These cattle believe they cannot do things. Because they believe they "can't," they have, instead of two feet, four feet now and one tail. Remember that. If anytime you say that you "can't," you are becoming like cattle.

The Dominant One

70

The Dominant One. This seventieth one is very beautiful. The Dominant One. The Dominant One was revealed to me when I was in California in the 1970's. A man was talking on television in the early morning about how man is powerful. He can change the surface of the earth, and he was laughing also and saying, "He can even pollute the earth, but he can send messages to the moon and stars." Then suddenly everything started to shake and he said, "I guess God is more powerful than anybody else." It was so strange.

Why did they not stop the hurricane with an atomic bomb? Why not? We are capable people. Why did they not spray something into the eye of the hurricane and blind the eye?

Who are you? When the earth is shaking, believe me, you are finished. You tremble. That is the Dominant One. From everything else, He is the Dominant One. He is the top.

What does this teach us? It is not because of God. God does not need these praises. Does He? Who cares about the praises of little ants like us? Who cares about man? But He cares for us because He is in us. Have you got it? He does not need these things. Who needs these things? We need them. We are going to be the Dominant One with our physical, emotional, and mental bodies, and we are going to use the energies and forces and matter that we have, goal-fittingly and intelligently, to reach a purpose.

Are you a Dominant One? Immediately when you see a bottle of whiskey, you take your crown and put it under your feet and bow to the bottle, to the cigarette, to the drugs, to the marijuana, to the sex, or to the dollars. You bow. You have lost your dominance. Be the Dominant One. Your body is your kingdom. You are going to dominate it. Your business is your kingdom. Your family is your kingdom. You are going to show spiritual dominance. Spiritual dominance is not forcing. It is your presence that is dominant.

Even if you cannot practice all that we said here, at certain times of crises in your life it pops into your mind and says, "You know, God's name is the Able One. There is nothing that is impossible. Come on. You are the Glorious One. You are the Noble One. You are the Beautiful One. You are the Self-Existing One. Do not depend on others." That is also a very great idea. The Self-Existing One does not lean on anybody; he or she leans only on God.

The Expediter

71

The Expediter, He Who Brings Things Forward. Out of Himself proceeded all that now exists, but that is not the end. This is a continuous process with new energies, new forms, new configurations, new successes. The more our consciousness expands, the more He brings out new revelations from His Treasury.

He is the source of all that exists and also the source of all that *will exist*. He is all-progressing, all-revealing. Every second a new light is revealed with new meaning and new significance. Like a river where every moment the ripples are different, His revelations are different and ever-flowing.

Of course, human beings must be like Him. We must bring forward everyday a new beauty, a new creativity, a new idea. We must be flowing like the river because our Source is Him. We must manifest Him throughout our whole life.

The Postponer

The Postponer. This is a very profound name. He delays things so that the cycles meet each other. This gives us a chance to develop our patience and faith in Him that all will happen at the right time.

In many things we hurry, but then we realize that if the things happened at the time we wanted it would have brought disaster to us. Because of events, we became a few minutes late and we escaped a big accident. A friend of mine was cursing and crying when he could not catch an airplane. Two hours later he called me to say that all the people on the plane were dead.

We must start to see God's Presence in many things and see that He postpones things for the good.

The First One

The First One. There was nothing before Him. There will be nothing after Him. The First One is always Him.

If we think that we were in existence with Him and are in existence with Him and will be in existence with Him always, such a concept takes a great pressure off our narrow consciousness and we live a better life.

Once when I was in school, after the athletic games were over, the Teacher said, "All of us must try to be the first, even if for some reason we cannot." God is always in everything and comes first because there was no one before Him. It is important that we let the First in us be recognized as the First. The First in us is the Self. All the rest in us must follow the First.

These names do not limit Him. They are reflections on the plane of our beingness. The more we advance, the more we see in these names. They are given to us to *remember Him.*

Remember your All-Self in your daily life and activities. You can repeat seven times daily any name and meditate on it.

The important point is that God must not disappear from our thoughts, words, emotions, actions. God must be present in our life, in churches, sanctuaries, temples. These words are to remember Him not in our head only but in our actions too.

Have you seen a bird that flies with one wing? You haven't? Why not?

There are two wings in the Universe, and these two wings are two states of consciousness. One state of consciousness is the consciousness of matter, of materialism — an earthly consciousness. The other consciousness is God consciousness. You must have these two consciousnesses to be able to fly, to live, and to relate things to each other.

If you only fuse with matter, eventually you become matter and you lose that Divinity in you that is giving consciousness and light and will and creativity and so on. But, also, if you are lost in God consciousness you become "spaced." You are not fit for anything on this earth. You go to a cave and sit there and get "spaced." This does not help.

We are here for one reason: to build a bridge between these two consciousnesses. That is a very serious saying. We must build a consciousness between our body and Soul, between our Divinity and our materiality. This is what we are doing. All education, all striving are to build a bridge between these two.

Sometimes we are not able to build this bridge. We start going higher, higher, building our bridge toward the highest. Then we turn back to our bodies again. When does this happen? When we use our divine consciousness, or our consciousness of Divinity, for our own self-interest, we reverse ourselves.

Some people start building the divine consciousness for their own self, ego, vanity, self-interest. That is not a bridge because that turns you back toward yourself. A bridge must be built that extends both ways. One way you are extending toward matter, toward the world, toward humanity, toward human problems. Then there is the other way which extends toward the spiritual values, toward the awareness of higher planes and contact with advanced centers of the Universe.

I was talking yesterday with somebody. He was so "spaced." He was in God already. I said, "You don't have one penny in your pocket. Do you realize that?" "Well," he said, "that is not important." "Really? How important was it to have a car and a little gas in it to get here? Do you see that?"

We teach these two ways. God knows what He is doing. He did not give us only one hand, one leg. We would look really strange like that. He gave two wings. Even our brain has two sides, left and right. Even our nose has two nostrils so that on one side we smell good smells of our neighbors and with the other we smell bad smells. It is so interesting!

These two consciousnesses — God consciousness and matter consciousness — are so important, and real disciples of the world or wise people, balanced people must start living in a balanced way. They must be successful in their life — good eating, good dressing, good houses, good cars. Why not? They are all important. And then, in the meantime, they must have a deepening consciousness.

What happens? See how interesting this is!

When you deepen your consciousness toward the divine light, you solve better the problems of matter. And if you really understand the mechanism, the causes and effects of the activities in matter, in the material world, you become able to express more and clearly the divine intent.

So, you bring these two seemingly opposite consciousnesses together and create one thing that we say is balance, equilibrium. If you achieve equilibrium in your life, you are the one who is successful, happy, and healthy because you are not one-winged.

Behind this symbolism there are lots of things. In your mind, think about it. For instance, how important it is to have a healthy body! But who is going to solve the problems of the body? —Only an elevated consciousness. And who is going to carry the plans and purpose of an elevated consciousness? —A healthy body.

In our Teachings we fly with both wings. We must be beautiful, but we must be also very advanced in our consciousness so that we have a very beautiful equilibrium and balance in our life.

In light of this we can see that humanity is mostly 99.9 percent lost in matter. For example, yesterday, how many hours did you think about God? Not even one person can say he did it for one hour. You did not. So what happened? You created an imbalance in your consciousness because your consciousness began to walk with one foot. Hopping does not work very well. You are going to be that divine consciousness so that you at least walk with two feet. Later, if you are really balanced, you can enter the Olympic games.

What I am saying is symbolic. You can enter more advanced racing, striving, progress if the two sides of yourself are really healthy. You can write a book about it. You can enter the highest path of striving and success and progress if you have two healthy feet, two sides of yourself. And that is the job of psychiatrists. What are psychiatrists going to do? They are going to see that that man is balanced! They give a tune-up. If he is angry, they give him an injection to numb him down. Anything they do is for one intention — to create balance.

Because we are thinking 99.9 percent about matter, it is very good that sometimes we turn our head and consciousness to the God consciousness and start developing at least 50, 60, 75, 80 percent God consciousness. If we develop God consciousness, we will see that our problems are more easily dissolved or solved with such a consciousness.

You can ask yourself, "Where is my consciousness focused?" Wherever your consciousness is focused, that is where your sickness is. You are without balance. For example, if your consciousness is totally focused in sex, all your troubles will come from sex, even your psychological problems. But if half of your consciousness is focused in your throat consciousness, which is creativity, you will balance the sex. Solar plexus and heart, kundalini and head center — these things balance you. In the future, scientists are going to create a balancing device or wisdom or science so that man creates balance in his consciousness, in his emotions, in his mind.

When you start creating, really fusing yourself in God consciousness, you will see that your physical, emotional, and mental bodies are illuminated with some light that helps your bodies act ideally. If you have that light within your body, your body is really light and beautiful.

Maybe you have had some experiences of this. For example, you listen to some beautiful music or a fantastic lecture or you see some paintings. After that, watch yourself. You are light. Have you had that experience? What happened? Your body is fused with a new, higher kind of energy. If you have God consciousness in you, you will see how your emotions and your mind are acting.

The other day I was talking with a young man. He said, "I can't translate this." "Why?" I said. "Because my mind is full of many, many things. I can't focus."

God consciousness cleans that, or at least minimizes it. When does it minimize? God consciousness minimizes when it fuses with your physical, emotional, and mental nature. You are a different man, a different woman. You are half light, half matter. That is all right. Then, you can increase the light if you want because your matter side is used as a vehicle for your Spirit, and the Spirit is used as a source of energy for the matter side of your being.

In everything try to reach a balance, and use not just one wing — the matter wing: money, money, money; sex, sex, sex; possessions and this and that. What about the other wing? Later you will see that this other wing is paralyzed and you cannot use it.

So this lecture is to create balance and to increase the light, the consciousness, the God consciousness within you.

Do you know what happens if you are God conscious? I will tell you a little story you may have already heard. A Teacher called ten little boys and said, "I am giving to each of you a little bird. Go and kill the bird, *but nobody must see it*! So each boy went somewhere, and eventually they killed their bird and came back. Too bad for the birds. They looked around and they were only nine boys. One boy was missing. They said, "Where is this boy?" Eventually the nine boys ran everywhere and found the boy with the bird still in his hand. The Teacher said, "Why didn't you kill this bird?" "Teacher," the boy said, "I didn't find anyplace that God cannot see." That is God consciousness!

If you start developing a little God consciousness — a little, little God consciousness like that boy — your actions will be totally different. You will see that you are hearing, you are seeing, you are aware of what is going on.

Because we say that our thinking cannot be observed, we can think the most obnoxious things. But if we create the awareness that our thoughts are recorded, our thoughts are observed, then we have a different behavior mentally. That is what the God consciousness is. God consciousness is to make you feel that God within you is observing everything you are doing, feeling, and acting.

Now there is another side of this that is interesting. Do you have computers? In the computer there is a place that says "Find." What are you going to find in all that accumulation of diskettes and hard disks? Let us say you want, for example, the word "Love." So you type "Love," then you push the buttons, then the computer goes everywhere and finds all that is related to "Love." This is an example of associative integration.

Your mind is a million times confused. To create certainty and balance in your mind, you will go through this process of *finding* things that are scattered in all the diskettes of your brain and bringing them into focus on "Love."

You see, for example you have a big bucket of screws and you are looking for one screw. You dump all the screws out, eventually, to find one. What are you doing? You are symbolically integrating those separate, scattered things into one association.

Now, all mental sicknesses are based in a confused mind that does not have integration and association. That is why a new psychological analysis is needed, and someone must write about this — how to create integrated thinking. The best way I found to integrate my mind was to take one word and work on that one word for six months so that I go through all the chains and circles and circuits of the diskettes in my mind, associate them, integrate them, align them, and make a chain that is substantial. I could touch every part of the chain.

Maybe you are surprised and wonder why I did that. My mind was very scattered — very! When I was seven years old, the Turks came and killed ninety-seven of our family in front of me, butchering them. Everywhere I was looking I was seeing them. I was going crazy.

One day I said to Mommy, "Things are everywhere." She came and hugged me and shouted to my Father, "Your son is going crazy." Of course I was. It was something that entered into my bones, and until now I have some times when it electrically hits me.

So I said I must find something to coordinate me. For ten, fifteen, twenty years, twenty-five years, I coordinated my computer, and I think it is a fine computer now — a masterpiece — because that computer wrote 125 books and hundreds of musical compositions. Can you imagine that? This computer is not scattered. It is aligned.

So with my experience I know that if you take one word and think about it, and if that word is about God, you are integrating, aligning, and compiling the divine sparks that are scattered within your nature.

When I talk to people they ask, "How did you learn these things? Where did you read them?" Believe me, I am the most reluctant reader. I think!

People talk. Even sometimes when I am counseling people, they talk and I listen to them, all the while I am thinking what they are saying is nonsense. They are not thinking!

Now let's integrate. By focusing your mind on the names of God you create balance, God consciousness. Second, you create integration and associative alignment within your mind. You can say any word you want — psychological, psychiatric, medical, electronic — but it is aligning. You create alignment within yourself. And third, with that light that comes with the integration, you can really control and manifest your actions in your best interest and in the best interest of all the people around you. Fourth, when you feel, when you organize your physical, emotional, mental mechanism as beautifully as you can, then you become a transmitter of the highest energies.

If you want to cultivate your spiritual nature, you must use it to balance your whole system. By thinking and talking about the names of God, you balance yourself. Your consciousness slowly starts operating within your spiritual nature instead of being imprisoned within your physical nature.

Now we come to more names of God.

The Last One

The Last One. I spent maybe one month on this word. One of the names of God is "The Last, the Last One, the Last." It is that Presence that is seeing your actions, feelings, your emotions, reactions, responses, and also totally aware of what you are thinking. My goodness, if I talk about it, it will be one book because it cleaned so many glamors and illusions in my mind.

What is "the Last"? When everything is dissolved, He is still there. For example, in Indian wisdom they say *Mahamanvantara, Mahapralaya* . . . . Everything comes and suddenly goes and disappears, and all forms dissolve in that great ocean, but the ocean is "the Last." Still it is there.

Your body goes. Later, your emotions go, your emotional body. Later, your mental body will disintegrate because it is also material, but *you* will remain. You will remain because you are *Him*.

So what happens if I have that consciousness? I have something in which I am anchored. I am not a boat floating in the ocean. I have an anchorage that

I am the Last. Even if everybody is lost, I am still there.

In the movie "Zorba the Greek," Zorba built something that was very successful, but then everything went down the drain. What did he do? He started to dance because he knew that he *is*. Do you understand this?

I was talking about this subject nearly thirty years ago. About ten days after speaking about it, a woman called me and said, "You don't know how thankful I am to you." I said, "What happened?" "Well," she said, "everything burned at my house, the car and furniture, everything, but I stood above all of it because of your lecture. I said, 'So what. It burned, but look! I am here!'"

Do you see the psychological effect of it? I like to talk about these things because they are not nonsense. They are really practical things, and they will help you. If suddenly everything is lost or a hurricane comes and takes the roof from your house and cleans it, do you know what some people do? They kill themselves or they fall into depression forever because their belongings *were* themselves. When their belongings are gone, symbolically, psychologically, they are gone. They do not exist anymore because *they are gone!* If you understand this, it helps you not to identify with your belongings. You are the Last or the Last One.

Someone's father died and he came and told me, "How grateful I am to you." I said, "Why?" "Because you taught us not to be depressed and broken and dead when someone dies." That's it! He is gone; but you are not him, you are not it because you know that you are the Last. Nothing will happen to you or to the one who left his body.[1]

It is so important to know that you are the Last and you are standing in your Divinity. Think about "the Last." Do some meditation for two, three, four minutes, and another day think more about it because it is your consciousness that controls you. Make your consciousness better and more powerful, and your life will be better and more powerful. That is the dynamo behind it.

---

1. See also *The Bhagavad Gita*, Ch. 2, tr. by author.

The Manifested One

The Manifested One. This name is so beautiful that I can give only little chips of it.

The whole Universe is something we think we can do anything we want with. We can destroy her oceans, lakes, rivers, her forests, even the mountains. We cheat them. We can do anything to Nature because all of it belongs to us. That is the illusion of Western philosophy. We think that the world and animals and everything are our property and we can do anything with them that we want. This is our gravest ignorance.

But look at what this name of God is saying. All of Nature is God. The trees are God. The rivers are God. The oceans are God. You are going to deal with them in a way that acknowledges that they are God. You do not open the sewage into the ocean because it is God. This name creates a different respect toward Nature which is the Manifestation.

You may know about this. There was a great philosopher, maybe 2700 years ago, who said, "In every atom there is the Divine Mind." The Mind of God is in every atom. The Greeks called it *nous*, and in Sanskrit it is called *mahat*. Mahat means the Mind that is in everything. People did not believe this, but now when they look at an atom they say, "Wow, what a dance is this in the atom. What energies, what kinds of configurations! It is like a solar system!"

Because that Mind is everywhere, in everything, you are going to respect that Mind and also respect the body of that Mind. If you really condition your consciousness in such a way that everything is a manifestation of God, of the body of God, how differently you would live.

If someone comes to you now and says, "I need your hair," and he shaves all your hair and puts it in his pocket, what do you do? You go crazy, of course, especially if you are so pretty and your hair is fantastic. What about when we are trimming all the hairs of the planet — the forests? Do you see what is happening? We are trimming without getting permission for what we are doing. We say, "Well, for our civilization it is good to do these things." We think so, but later it reacts and destroys us because the Manifestation becomes sick of us and wants to clean us.

The same is true of the inner God. This body, this heart, this brain is your manifestation, and you are going to deal with them as God within you. As God within you, you are going to deal with your nature in such a way that you respect it as the highest manifestation of God. That is when you will become really successful in your life.

If you abuse yourself, for example by using drugs, coffee, black tea, marijuana, cigarettes, and other trash, what are you doing? You are throwing mud at the face of God that is within you.[1]

You are going to respect yourself highly — your body, your emotions, your mind. You are going to respect these configurations, these forms to such a degree that you do not work against your own interest and destroy the machine that is given to you. What if you had a teenager and you bought for him the most beautiful car, but the next day you came and saw that he had taken a big hammer and destroyed it?

Your body, your heart, your mind are the manifestations of God. You are going to be so careful that the gifts that are given to you will remain in the best shape possible.

Your mind is a masterpiece. I was traveling to New York, and some computer genius was sitting by me. He said, "You know, we created greater things than the mind." I wanted to be dramatic, so I laughed loudly. Immediately the stewardess ran to me and said, "What do you want?" I said, "I want a cup of water to pour on this man!" "What?" he said. I said, "You are crazy. Who created the computer?"

You have a mind that is still, I can say, only working seventeen percent. If your mind starts to

---

1. For a detailed look at how drugs affect our bodies for many lifetimes, see the author's video "Why Drugs Are Dangerous."

work one hundred percent, you will be God conscious. You will not need your television and radio and telephone because all are for a lack of bridging. What is the telephone? It shows you cannot bridge. Television? You cannot bridge. You will be so perfect that your inner center will do a better job than your telephones or televisions do.

If you read, for example, the *Bhagavad Gita,* you will find that Sanjaya is sitting by a blind king and the king says, "Can you tell me what is happening in the battlefield?" Sanjaya says, "Well, now, two armies are lined up against each other, and Krishna is taking Arjuna between the armies so that he observes and sees what is happening in the armies." Sanjaya was seeing clairvoyantly. He did not need television because he worked through the God consciousness within himself.

We have become materialized to such a degree that we have lost our Divinity within ourselves. Now is the time for giving the names of God to bring ourselves back to the consciousness of Divinity, to God consciousness. Try to see this week if you have five or six minutes of God consciousness.

How can I say most simply what God consciousness is? God consciousness is an ever-inclusive consciousness. Does that make sense? God consciousness is the deepest humility consciousness. Humility . . . . When you see people with ego and vanity, you know that they ate too much matter and they became fat. You "eat" matter. If you "ate" divine substance, you would become humble. And the third explanation of God consciousness is the deepest gratitude. If you take these three, you have a good definition of God consciousness.

See if you have such a consciousness within you tomorrow, next day, this week. Later you will see that the Hierarchy has this device, and later computer geniuses are going to make a device and we are going to program it and see that whenever we are God conscious it will record and we will see that Tuesday it is one minute because something very horrible came to you and you said, "God . . . !" If the horrible thing did not come, God is not there even. You are going to see how much God consciousness you have.

For example, people say "Krishna consciousness," "Christ consciousness." They are all beautiful, fantastic. I love them! Don't forget, we are inclusive. But God consciousness is deep.

Q&A

> *Question: When you spoke about taking a name and finding the associations, it sounded like we are to take from our experience, from how we feel. When you take the name into meditation, are you looking for new things instead of past experience?*

Answer: I will give you a very simple example. If you have a lake on which the trees are reflected, unless that lake is clean, there is no reflection. First you are going to clean the circuits of your system — taking out and trying and seeing with what this word is associated. Even in your mind there are lots of explosive sections. Pay attention to this very carefully.

If you have a chain of thought, some of the links in that chain are very explosive. And those explosive links really create devastation in your system. For example, let us say that ten years ago or fifty years ago you witnessed how a man took a knife and said "God!" and killed someone. That is an explosive ring in your chain for the word "God." Now, what are you doing? You are thinking about the word "God." You go and find this church, that church, this book, that book. Suddenly a leak comes there. It was hidden there, and it was devastating your life without your knowledge. It came to the surface and you clean it.

What we are talking about is not hocus-pocus. It is not religion. It is science. If you use these things, you will see how beautiful they are. I found these things by seeing what is happening to me.

For example, by thinking about fifty names, every three months one name, I cleaned all the chains where I found explosive rings. I brought them out, examined them, cleaned them, analyzed them, trashed them, and finished with them. I changed them.

> **Question:** *Is there a distinction when you think of the names and when you "sit in" them?*

Answer: Yes, but the first thing is to reach it, catch it, and "eat" it. So it is the same process but different stages. You need all of them. First you think. Then you become a little impressed. Then you start assimilating. Then you become it. That is how the light penetrates slowly, slowly, and imbues your whole system. It does not happen immediately. You must ask for it. Thinking is asking. Then meditation is assimilating — chewing and swallowing, then becoming *it*. You see, these are different stages.

> **Question:** *Can you talk about what happens when we focus on something such as a sickness?*

Answer: The sickness, the trouble will be in the place upon which you concentrated. For example let us say that you are totally concentrated on your sex.

All your astral, etheric, and mental energies will go to that center. That center will enjoy it tremendously until one day you see that that center cannot take anymore. What happened? Degeneration started in that center. Then the glands degenerate. Then the organs degenerate. That is the whole thing.

You are going to take the pressure into another center. I am not saying that sex is bad. Don't misunderstand me. I am not against sex. I am saying you must have balance, you must balance yourself. If you are eating potatoes everyday, God save you!

Women know better than men about these things. I am sorry to say that, but it is right. Women know the limits of sex, of everything. If men listen, the women can be a balancing factor in their life. You see, you are going to balance each other. Also, woman and man are like wings.

Question: Can these explosive rings also be karmic?

Answer: Yes, of course. Everything is karmic. There is nothing in your nature that you did not create. Don't kid yourself. You are responsible for everything you have either by being positive or being negative, either by being neutral or active. You see, people think that karma is built if you do something, if you say something, if you take something. This is general information that people sell to each other. Karma is built, heavily, when you do not talk, when you do not do, when you do not think, when you do not serve. "When you do not" creates more karma than when you do because "not doing" is "doing" subjectively. If you can understand this, then that is enough!

In summary, you take one of the names of God and meditate on it, think about it, so that you discover the deeper meanings of that name. Your meditation can be deeper if you have lots of experiences in your life, or if your consciousness begins to work on higher dimensions and more inclusively.

Sometimes during your meditation you meet certain explosive chains of associations which temporarily stop your progress. For example, if you are thinking about *the Last One*, you may suddenly feel a rejection from inside. What can happen is that you had in the past a bad association with that word. Suppose you were waiting to enter a party and the guard said, "You are *the last one*. You will not have a chance to join the party," and this caused lots of anxiety in you. The anxiety may return every time you think of that word until you clean it.[1]

---

1. See *The Subconscious Mind & the Chalice* for further information on subconscious recordings.

The names of God is a very interesting concept in my mind. In olden times when people were not educated and they were just starting their mental evolution, they used to call everything God. Something that they did not understand was called God. For example, they did not understand what fire was, so they called it God. They did not understand the wind, how it was coming and going and then becoming still. They would say, "It is God." If something happened in their life and they did not know the cause of it, they called the cause God. Everything was God. The river was God. The lake was God. The ocean was God. The flowers were God. Everything was God. Something that was mysterious and beautiful was God.

Then what happened? As mental evolution and expansion started, great Initiates and wise people started to say that God is in all and in everything. Then they said that God is in everything. Eventually they said that there is nothing else but God. Look how interesting it is. The most advanced and the most primitive people were saying the same thing.

What is the cause of our finding names of God and calling Him different names from different experiences? It is a Presence in us and in Nature. God is trying to create responses, to evoke responses from us toward him. And that God that is in Nature and within us is trying to define that feeling that we are having about God.

For example, if you call God "Almighty," that is a concept in your mind. That is a feeling you have about Him. That concept, that idea, that feeling within you was created as you responded to His pull, to His magnetism, to His attraction through which He was trying to reveal Himself. In this process you were creating bridges to understand Him. These bridges are nothing else but names. For example you say, "You are beautiful." It is a bridge to communicate. I want to express my feeling about you, my response to you, my ideas about you, my concepts about you, and I say, "You are really beautiful." Maybe you are not beautiful to others, but you are beautiful to me because I wanted to bridge myself with you and understand you and make you understand that I am feeling beautiful about you. You are beautiful in me. In my concept, in my estimation, in my appreciation, you are beautiful.

The names of God are nothing else but bridges to something that is beyond our conception. As we progress and find more responses and more communication with that Mysterious Presence within us and within Nature, we change the names. Each name becomes a way, a path through which we approach the mystery which we are calling by a name.

It is not that we are creating God. I have read many, many books that said, "God does not exist. We created Him." That is a very false concept. If nothing exists, you do not respond to it. It is a vacuum. There should be something that you respond to. Our giving a name for God proves that there is something there, but we are seeing It from ten million miles away. We are calling It a flower. Then we are calling It a star. Then we are calling It a Galaxy. Then according to our feeling, thinking, and subjective experiences, we give different names to It.

One day my Teacher said that if you research the roots of the names of God, given by various nations, you will find that the most prevalent idea of God was Fire. We even read in the Bible that God spoke through fire, and He was "a Consuming Fire."

There is a verse in *The Bhagavad Gita* which shines as a diamond of all-inclusiveness. Let people call Him by any name. Let people approach Him in any way. He will reward them. It says, "In whatever way men approach Me, in the same way, I reward them. In all their ways of worship, men follow My path."[1]

---

1. *The Bhagavad Gita 4:11,* tr. by the author.

But whether you say, "I know Him," or you say, "I do not know Him," He is there. That is why you are talking about Him. There is a Presence there that is reflecting within you in the form of certain ideas, certain concepts, certain opinions. These opinions, ideas, and concepts do not matter because they are the reflection in you and you are reflecting that reality *according to what you are*, how progressed you are, how open you are, how understanding you are. As your understanding is growing and growing and growing, you are saying, "God is Mind." Then you are saying, "God is Universal Cosmic Consciousness." As you are expanding your mind and your consciousness, the reflection of God within your system is changing. That system is nothing else but naming God. You are naming God. You are naming your feeling, thought, Intuition about the Presence.

Sometimes try to go over the names of God, whether you understand or not.

Each name given to God is a seed thought for meditation. For example we say, "Almighty One." What does it mean — Almighty One? Let us say that this is a picture that came into your mind, and you did not find any other words to define your feeling, your concept, except Almighty One. Analyze what Almighty One means to you. Even if you do not know whether He exists or not, your thinking about the Almighty One will create new responses and new relationships with the One you are thinking about under the name of Almighty One, even though He can be something else.

We are not talking on the kindergarten level. We want to stretch your mind a little so that you do not remain on the level of the devotee saying, "God, give me something," but you do not know to Whom you are speaking.

Another interesting thing happened in the progressive course of humanity. Angels were called God. If people saw an angel, they said, "That is God." Especially in the Middle East and Far East the people called devas or spirits "god." "God came and spoke to me." One day an Indian told me that God came and spoke to him. It was an angel, a deva, a spirit or ancestor that came to him, and he called it God. This God became bigger and bigger until it became a national God. Eventually it became the power of the planet that creates all this planetary beauty we have — rivers, winds, waterfalls, birds, animals, trees, fruits, and flowers. It is all beautiful. That is the God of our planet.

When we expanded our consciousness a little more, God became the power that created the Solar System. What is happening in the Solar System? A sun and twelve planets for millions of years are producing this beauty, this symphony, this life. As we became a little more advanced, we said that this Galaxy is God. The Galaxy is ensouled by a Life, and that Life was God for us because we did not see beyond the Galaxy. Now that we are seeing beyond the Galaxy, we are saying that God is something that has no beginning and no end and has no measure. He is there, everywhere, in everything. Then we are coming to the understanding that God can never be known except if He is with us because He is the Knower.

So when we talk about the names of God, don't understand that God has names. God does not have names. It is even wrong to say that God has names because if you say that God has names, you are limiting God. How can a Limitless One enter into your brain. He is an Ocean! You cannot pour the ocean into your "cup" here. The cup is small. He is beyond everything — so He has no name. But . . . all names are proofs that we have a *contact* with something that exists.

And to define that feeling of "Oh, God!" means to build a bridge between you and Him and also to build a bridge between your real and unreal self. Not only are you knowing Him; also you are knowing yourself. Actually, the process is this. You will never know Him until you know yourself because by knowing yourself you will, in the microscopic stage, see Him reflected within you. Everything that is in Him is within you in a seedling stage. When you find your Core, your Inner Essence, you will have different, different concepts about Him that surpass all your former understanding.

A lady came to me and said, "I do not know to whom I am praying." I gave a wholesale answer. I said, "You pray. He will listen, whatever He is, wherever He is. He is the Listener."

There is a name for God which is "the Ear." God is the Ear. Imagine an ear. It is such a comic name for God, but if you search to the bottom of it, you will understand one thing — God hears everything. Can you say that God does not hear everything if He is Almighty, and so on? You go deeper and deeper and say, "God hears everything." Then you come to your senses. That is the shock. If God is going to hear everything, what am I doing all day and night — yak-yakking and gossiping and hating and cursing? What am I doing?

So, why am I giving you this example? It is to make you see that what we are saying is not hallucination. It is not only abstract. It is also very practical.

God sees everything. So what? God sees everything. Now we philosophically, scientifically understood that God is everywhere and sees everything. If we stop there, we are not making our teaching practical. Then one day when I am in the market I extend my hand and steal a watch. As I steal the watch, it comes to my mind that God sees everything. "Oh. I'd better put it back! If He is seeing everything, I don't want to steal it."

So this teaching has an abstract dimension which is there to expand our consciousness and also a practical dimension to use that teaching, that light that we are receiving from this teaching, in our individual behaviors and relationships.

But one thing that you must never forget is this — that every name we are talking about here is given on our levels. If our level is a Fifth Degree Initiate, a Master, we will talk about these names of God but in higher dimensions.

For example, your child asks you, "Mommy, what is this tree?" You say, "This tree gives fruit. God created it, and we eat the fruit and become strong." Now that is your answer. It is not a wrong answer. It is an answer that meets the level of the understanding of the child.

When you are talking to a scientist, you can talk about one leaf for hours — how that leaf transforms the energies from the Sun and this and that. Your answer is different. It is the same tree, the same God, but your explanation and understanding and relating of your understanding to others is on a totally different level.

So, how can you find that different level? This is the most important thing. First, we have the presence, the abstract presence. Second, we have the practical side of it. Third, the process of it.

What is the process of it so that you go from the practical to the abstract? There is a bridge lacking here, you see. For example you say, "We need some medicine." OK, you know the formula, and you have all the practical things to make it, but you do not know how to do it.

How to do it is meditation upon the names of God. When you are meditating and pondering and going deeper and deeper into the names of God, you are surpassing the level that was taught to you and you are finding new levels where you do not need to learn. You are granted certain revelations.

And there is a fourth part that is very interesting. When you are experiencing, your experience is formulating a name for your experience. For example, you lick some sugar. If you don't know what sweetness is, you eventually say, "It is sweet." By saying "sweet" you are not defining what sugar is. It is a chemical compound; it is energies, etc., but you are giving it a name to pinpoint it, to remember that you are talking about sugar and sweetness.

Now I will go to the names.

The Internal One

The Internal One. In many Middle Eastern and Far Eastern scriptures He is called the Internal One, the One Who is Internal. As you search for it you can see that it is deeper than what you found. Then you dig a little more, and it is deeper than what you found, and then deeper. When you find it, you find your Self. Isn't that something?

The Internal One. The Deeper One. For example, you think, "This is me. This is my nose, my ears." But that is *not* the Deeper One. Where is the True One? The Deeper One that is the Cause of your existence, the cause of your seeing, hearing, speaking, thinking, meditating, analyzing, synthesizing, reasoning. That is the Deeper One. For example you say, "I am the speaker." When you go to the real speaker behind it, there is another speaker, another thing, another thing that is so deep! Eventually when you go to the deepest there and the deepest within you, eventually the two hands meet and you say, "My Father and I are One." See what Christ was saying?

If you understand only the surface meaning of these words, you will never understand anything because all these words are nothing else but X, Y, Z — X, number; Y, length; and Z, depth. You are just saying algebraic names to mean something else, but X does not mean anything. For example X can be for the number of people. You say, "I had X number of people in the meeting." X number of people can be ten thousand or two million. It stands for something, but it does not say what it is.

We must eventually have an experience of the Presence, an experience of God. This is not an experience of seeing an angel or hearing a voice, but an experience that He is within you. You are within Him, all your thoughts, feelings, actions, are His thoughts, feelings, and actions. You realize that He is in everything, in everybody. He is the Presence, and you live in that Presence within you, awake or asleep, whether you are dead or alive.

So think about these things — the Internal One. We have many internal things. For example, we have our body. Behind our body there is the emotional body which we cannot see sometimes. That is the Internal One in comparison to our physical life. Then we go a little deeper and we can find the thinking there. It is the Internal One. When we dig into the thinking, we can find the motives. Then we go a little deeper and find some Presence there Who is the Internal One beyond our physical, emotional, and mental natures. The same thing is in the Universe. We have all these outside things, and we have deeper things in Nature that we do not know. All these deeper things and outer things are manifested as persons, as lives.

This is maybe a new concept for you, but it is so interesting. When you are talking about your emotions, do you know what your emotions are? Every emotion is an electrical wave, and that wave is composed of millions of little lives, emotional lives. It is a living Universe!

You see, we say "humanity" as a whole, but what is humanity? These billions, billions, billions of people are building humanity. So "Internal" is beyond what you see. If your seeing changes, you start seeing deeper things. Still, whatever you are seeing, there is a depth behind it . . . until you reach to your Self, until you reach to God and face Him. That is why a disciple said, "We see ourselves in a mirror, but later we see ourselves face to face." I had a hard time understanding this. You can see yourself in the mirror and say, "That is me." But what does it mean later to see yourself face to face? That was an experience that a great disciple had. We do not have it yet, but he had it and he recorded that there is a state of consciousness or an experience in which man comes face to face with himself.

You have some experiences. For example, you lie. Then you go home and say to yourself, "You know, you are lying and lying." This is face to face confronting yourself, but still it is your ugly face. It is not the Divine Face behind you. So the Invisible One, the Interior One is the One you always try to reach. The beautiful thing is that as you try to reach the Internal One you transform. You become more beautiful, you become more loving, you become purer, you become more creative because the closer you go to Him, the closer you go to the interior section of your beingness. You are becoming like God.

The Internal One, is the dynamic part of the bodies, the Spirit, the One Who puts into motion the body, the emotions, the mind in a controlled way. The deeper we think on the Internal One, the closer we go to our own essence. God is the Internal One in every form, from the atom to the Galaxy.

Each name that is given to God is a name that you eventually must adopt, and that is the power of it. For example you say, "the Enlightened One, the One Who is Light." OK, that is a challenge. Every name is a challenge for you because every name of God was a challenge for somebody who experienced it.

You see the Enlightened One, the Light, the Light of the World, the Light of the Universe. What kind of light are you? Can you one day say, "Millions of years later people will tell me that I was the Light of the World"? For example, they called Buddha "the Light of the East, the Light of Asia." They called Christ "the Light of the West." How did They become Light? Well, They were feeling that there was a Light and that They should be the Light itself.

Religion is not outside in the books. Religion is an inner mechanism, an inner laboratory, an inner factory in which you feel these things, you actualize these things, and eventually you touch the mystery behind the outside world. This name is a challenge. We can go for hours and hours. Actually, if I retire when I am a hundred years old, I will sit and write a book for each name. Yes, it is possible. For me, there is nothing impossible.

The Governor

The Governor — the One Who governs. One day I asked my Daddy, "What is it that governs our body?" "What do you mean?" he asked. "How come I am moving, I am feeling, I am thinking? Who governs all these things?" "Well," he said, "we will talk about it."

It is very interesting. Who is governing you? Is it your stomach? Is it your sex? Is it your bank book? Is it your dollar? Is it your fear? Is it your subconscious urges and drives, hypnotic suggestions?

So, we come from this reasoning — that there is something that without that something, nothing is governed.

And what does it mean "to govern"? Look at how interesting it is. To govern means to regulate the lives of all available forms according to the laws and existing principles of the Universe. For example, you do not move your hand without any reason. There must be a reason to do something, and the Interior One, that One Who is governing you, is calculating everything and then doing an action. For example, if you are talking about something, that talking is not coming from your nose and going out of your mouth. You have reasoning. You have logic. You are feeling. You are calculating things. You are co-measuring things . . . and *then* you are talking.

So to govern means to relate people together in such a way that they head for one purpose and for the actualization of one plan that is good for them. Or, to govern means to bring people together in such a way that you reveal the beauties of each one better than if each were alone.

For instance, I have piano notes. If I govern these notes, bring them together with meaning and plan, they will be a song, a symphony, something great. That is what to govern means.

Another explanation — To govern means to harmonize and lead all forms to those destinations where they will slowly, slowly see the oneness of life within themselves. It is so beautiful to govern.

We feel that there should be a central command within us to make our mind to think, our emotions to feel, and our hands and feet to move. To govern means to coordinate all our systems to fulfill a plan, to perform an act, and to reach a purpose.

To govern means to organize all available forms according to their laws and principles in order to actualize a personal, group, and a global plan.

To govern means to relate to people in such a way that each one has more possibilities to transcend himself, to actualize his potentials, and to offer them for a group purpose.

That is what, seemingly, God does. Life as a whole is organized and related in such a way that all living forms are unfolding themselves eventually to actualize His Purpose.

To govern means to let people unfold their consciousness to such a degree that they are able to benefit from the forces, energies, and laws of the Universe to discover their divine Reality.

You have many governors within you. There are small and big governors. Your etheric centers are governors. Your heart is a governor. It goes poom, poom, poom to regulate your blood. Your mind is a governor. You go to your office and put everything in the right place, which means you are arranging your life in such a way that you fit yourself for a greater purpose than what you are at present. Think about how the Governor is governing this whole Creation. It is such a beautiful idea.

You see, when you are thinking about the names of God, you are expanding your consciousness toward the Infinite. How is this Solar System running in the air, in space? How are the millions of Solar Systems running? Why are they not hitting, beating each other and finishing everything? Who is governing all these energies, all these forces, all these laws and principles? How are they governed so that the whole stands as a whole, as a beautiful mechanism that runs faultlessly and without any friction?

This is why, when people started to think about God, they eventually reached a concept that they translated by the word "Governor." They did not find anything else to explain it. They said, "God governs, so He is a Governor, the Supreme Governor." But to reach there you need millions of years of experience and education so that you eventually can translate that feeling, that concept into the word "Governor."

For example, if you have a computer, you push an "A" on the keyboard. "A" is not a value. "A" presents a symbol, and that "A" goes through all the electronic channels and makes, eventually, a concept on the monitor screen. In the same way, when you are thinking about the Governor, that Governor is slowly, slowly making a deeper impression in your mind that there should be something that puts everything in harmony in relation to the Purpose and the Plan. That something is "God" according to your experiences. You see how beautiful it is?

The Most Exhalted One

78

The Most Exalted One. One cannot create such a name except if he has had an inner revelation, an intuitive perception about Him.

You see, they did not find any other word! The Most Exalted One. They said, for example, "This sergeant is so beautiful." Then they saw the king. "Wow, this king is an exalted one." Then they saw the king of kings. "Oh, he is more exalted." Then maybe they saw the Planetary Logos. They said, "He is the Exalted One." Then they saw the Solar Logos. They said, "Ah, the Exalted One!" Then they saw the Galactic Logos. "Ooo, what is He? He is beyond all this exaltation. He is the most, the highest Exalted One" — because they can't say anything else.

You see, the names that we give to God are the measure of our ignorance. Eventually, eventually when you know God, do you know what you will do? You will keep your mouth shut. Somebody will ask you, "Tell me about God." "What can I tell you? Who are you to understand God?"

One day I asked my Teacher, "Where is God?" He just looked at me. Then I asked, "Who is He?

Explain to me." He shrugged and waved his hand toward the space. He is not the Santa Claus that you are making Him to be. He is not! You see the greatness of God is His namelessness. Are we contradicting what we are saying? No. Names are necessary to define our steps. If you are going from here to Los Angeles, every step on the map is 200 miles, 300 miles, 360 miles. Now we are passing this place, that place. It is all phenomena. It is all measured by our mind to convey to us that we are not in the same places. We are going to someplace else. But, wherever we go we are only on the earth. Do you understand this comedy?

Most Exalted One. What is exaltation? If somebody asked, what would we say? Exaltation is like this, for example: you have a heater and heat is coming out. You go and touch it and say, "Wow, the heat is there." Exaltation is feeling the presence of God. And when you feel the presence of God, you become an exalted one because you have a heat in you. Do you understand? It is a little example but these little examples pave the way to deeper understanding.

Each name can be a path leading us to His Presence. Each name can create locations within us where we worship Him when He touches us. The exaltation of our Spirit is caused by the feeling of His Presence. In exaltation we feel that we have made a contact with Him.

The Devoted One

The Devoted One. This was so interesting for me. The seventy-ninth name of God, according to the scriptures, is the Devoted One. I said, "No . . . I can be devoted to something, you can be devoted to something, or we can all be devoted to something, but to whom is He devoting Himself?" Well . . . then I found a way to understand. Is a mother devoted to the child? Where did he go? How is he doing? What is happening? Is he married? Is he divorced? The Devoted One. Devotion means that, day and night, you are in His Mind and He is trying to make you like Him. That is devotion.

Now you can find something else here that is very practical. When you think that nobody loves you, you are going to commit suicide, you have no friends, everything is lost, think at that moment that there is a Devoted One. He is devoted to you. When you do that, you release yourself from your darkness. The Devoted One loves you so much. He loves you deeper than anyone else does. He loves you. He is devoted to you. He not only loves you, He also sacrifices everything possible. Everything is for you.

Go and take them — greater enlightenment, great revelations. He is devoted. For millions of ages we were atoms. Now we are thinking people. How much devotion was necessary to make a "cabbage" into a human being? It is very deep if you think about it. How much devotion is necessary by that Creator to make a little worm into a scientist, into a Lincoln, into a Beethoven? See what devotion means!

We know that God is Devotion, the Devoted One. What about us? If we have the same Essence within us, how much must we be devoted? And to what? — To Him that is within us! Is that what they are doing in Herzegovina? the Middle East? Africa? the Far East? They are butchering each other.

To whom are you going to be devoted? If you want to be entering into the Path that will lead you to God, to becoming a God, you are going to become devoted, devoted to each other, devoted to the Life, devoted to the trees, the bunnies, the birds. But we are not devoted. That is why we are remaining far away from God. And the further we stay away, the more sorrows and pains and destruction we will have.

Devoted One. Are you devoted to your husband, to your wife, to your children, to your friends, to your Teachers, to your servants? If you are not devoted, you cannot become like Him because He is Devotion. Do you see how every name is creating different ideas?

It is very interesting that every pain and suffering is the lack of devotion, is the result of the lack of devotion. So, you are going to be devoted. But to be devoted does not mean to surrender yourself to a thief that is cutting your throat. Do not misunderstand me.

Acceptor of Repentance

The *Acceptor of Repentance*. This is very beautiful. Isn't that an interesting name? Acceptor of Repentance. If you repent, He accepts it. He does not say, "Now you know your mistakes, now you realize, and now you are going to sit in the electric chair and be cooked." He does not say that. He says, "I accept your repentance," and He gives you a chance because He was the One Who made the mistake within you. He wants to release Himself. Do you see that? That is acceptance.

Whenever you repent, it means three things. First, you know that you made a mistake. Second, you go and pay for your mistake to your friend — at least with your words, with your hugs. Third, you decide not to repeat your mistake again. That is repentance. If you do that, why not give a chance to you?

Repentance is a long process of education to make you understand that you are doing something wrong to other people and to yourself. Then, when you understand that you stole fifty dollars, you pay it back. You cannot repent without paying it back.

Then you decide with all your firmness, "I do not want to be doing these things again." If you do that, there is acceptance. You can do it by yourself. You do not have to confess to anybody. You made some mistakes. Know exactly what you did, pay them back, and then say, I am not going to do them again. Then you will see that you are accepted.

Now look how beautiful this is. To be accepted means to build a bridge between you and your Soul, then a bridge between your Soul and God. You are accepted. You are not fragmented anymore. In every mistake that you make, you become fragmented. You feel aloof, isolated, left alone, abandoned. With every mistake you make, you feel these things. But when you repent you bridge the gaps, the cleavages, and eventually you become whole within yourself and you become whole with God, with that Mysterious Something in the Universe. You feel it. Immediately as you feel it, you are healthier, happier, and more prosperous.

So, never say that you are guilty. Never, never, never! Never think about the past when you did something stupid. You did it. It is finished! But repent for it, and decide not to repeat it again. Then pay it back as fast as you can. If you are smart, you will not say, "*Mañana.* Next incarnation." That is the heavy part. Whether we like it or not, we are going to pay it.

These names are so delicious. If you get involved in them, you are going to go deeper and deeper.

Repentance really means to turn your face away from your lower self, which means that you no longer spend time and energy following the deeds of your lower self. Instead, you dedicate yourself to the goals of your Soul.

The Avenger

The Avenger — the One Who inflicts punishment. God avenges in three ways:

First, He expands your consciousness and enlightens you in such a way that you see your mistakes, and thus He gives you a chance not to repeat them.

Second, He prevents you from progressing on the Path of Illumination if you do not repent. He watches you and makes it more difficult for you to meditate, to study, to strive as long as your motives are not right. For example, the authorities prevent you from holding higher positions if your life is not clean. Most people are surprised when they do not like to do meditation. If they would check their life, they would see that they live a life contradictory to the life which meditation tries to actualize. The Divine Avenger exists not to punish you but to bring you in line or to bring you back into the Light.

Third, He urges you through your Soul to pay back for the harm you did.

In our human system, punishment means to cause pain and suffering because of moral failures.

But in its esoteric meaning, to avenge means to make a person work for God instead of for evil, to make a man serve instead of exploit others, to make a man serve his Higher Self instead of his lower self. In the Gospel, we have a good example. Paul was persecuting Christians, but God made him preach about Christ.

The Tolerant One

The Tolerant One. He cares for your bodily needs, emotional needs, mental needs, and spiritual needs. If you fail in your duties and responsibilities, He does not immediately cast you into hell. He waits. Even though He knows that you have made mistakes, He waits. He cares for you when you did anything from ignorance.

We must remember that His outstanding nature is love and fire. Fire purifies you. Love attracts you closer to Him. In tolerance you see the reasons why a person fails, but you still see the possibilities for his regeneration and achievement and you do not deprive him of that chance.

The Consoling One

The Consoling One. Whenever you open your heart to Him and reveal the condition of your life, your body, your heart, your mind and ask Him to bring harmony, peace, and serenity into your system, into your heart, you feel His consoling power, His soothing power.

Whenever it becomes impossible for you to forgive yourself for the deeds you did, for the emotions you had, for the vices you demonstrated, and for the thoughts you thought, He consoles you.

He consoles you by illuminating your mind, your heart; by strengthening your nervous system; by showing you the endless paths of possibilities, the reasons and causes of what happened in your life. Then He energizes you in order for you to overcome your weaknesses.

Consolation is a state of peace in which the chaos of your life begins to turn into harmony, into hope, into the vision of the future.

Be with Him, and He will console you if you have lost a beloved one, if you have failed in many ways. He is there to challenge you to start again. His consolation is energy, inspiration, striving from your heart.

The Power

The Power — the Controlling Power, the Unconditioned. Can you imagine reaching a stage in which you are not *conditioned* but are *Self-conditioned* and *Self-sufficient*, where all life experiences throughout millions of years have been leading you? In total fusion with the Power, one reaches absolute freedom.

Individuals, groups, nations, and eventually all of humanity must, step by step, reach freedom. Freedom is carried on only through synthesis and unification. Some leaders of humanity do not see that. They think that cooperation and unification deprive them of their freedom. But in reality, freedom can only be achieved by the unification of all levels.

The Power is not an individual but the sum-total of those who have achieved freedom.

The Lord of Majesty

The Lord of Majesty, Glory, Honor. The Lord of Majesty means to have power over all energies, all laws. The Lord of Glory means to be the expression of unlimited beauty. The Lord of Honor means to be fully recognized by all sentient beings, including all Intelligent Directors in the Universe.

In thinking about the Lord of Majesty, Glory, and Honor, one slowly develops his soul tendencies and strives to make his life majestic, glorious, honorable. Such a striving helps one avoid falling into traps that lead him into miserable and lamentable conditions of life.

The Balancing One

86

The Balancing One — the Power that has the capacity to balance spirit and matter, cause and effect, destruction and regeneration in all domains of life. Actually there will be no existence, no progress in the Universe without balancing.

Creation and dissolution, existence and non-existence, all are phenomena of balance. Balance exists in atoms as in the highest Galaxies. Without balance, all turns into chaos.

How important it is to cultivate balance in all our actions, emotions, words, and thoughts! Co-measurement leads to balance. One cannot practice love and compassion without balance. Unity and synthesis are based on balance.

The Collector

87

The Collector — One Who brings His parts of creation closer to each other, closer in understanding, closer in feeling, closer in knowing, closer in cooperating. His Hands are everywhere, His Eyes are everywhere. His Love surrounds all that will bring us together. All the family will be united.

In time and space, parts of His manifestation can stay apart from the whole, but as life continues He collects them under His Wings. To stay apart is to live in pain and suffering; to stay as One is to live in bliss. His gathering is gradual and takes millions of years. All His children eventually turn to their Home.

The Independent One

The Independent One. The only criterion of independence is to be the Only Existing One. There is nothing else but God. *Tat Tvam Asi.*

It is in Oneness that divine independence is realized. Those who realize the Divinity within themselves experience independence. Independence is achieved by cultivating the divine potentials within us to be self-sufficient.

It is through becoming divine that one becomes independent. To be divine means to manifest light, love, and power gradually on higher levels and with greater effectiveness.

Everyone faithful to the Lord must develop spiritual, pure independence.

Bestower of Wealth

Bestower of Wealth — material, emotional, mental, spiritual. All that belongs to Him can belong to you, even without *karma*. There is nothing that He cannot do for you to have wealth.

The real wealth is His Presence within us, is His identity with us. When we commune with Him, His wealth on all levels floods our life.

We must be grateful for all the blessings that we have — for our physical, emotional, mental, and spiritual wealth — because they are His Presence within us, and we must deal with His Presence to increase His Glory within us.

The Restrainer

The Restrainer. For every level, for every occasion and condition, there exist limits. If you try to break a limit without outgrowing it, you are restrained. You are brought back to your normal speed. Many Laws of Karma restrain you in various ways so that again and again you will be in a condition which you created by your labor and achievements.

We see in history how individuals, groups, nations, even races are restrained and put under discipline when they violate the Laws of Love, Light, and Beauty. By restraining the units, He makes them find new footings to climb again toward the summit. When God restrains humanity through a natural calamity, He does not pollute the earth, the air, but creates a new opportunity for advancement.

The Distresser

The Distresser. Everyone of us has experienced in certain moments the interference of a feeling or a thought or a spark of Intuition which has caused us to wait a moment and review what we are doing. In such moments we are distressed because we feel fear, we feel doubt about the things we are doing, saying, thinking, or feeling. Such an experience repeats in us after we go ahead and do all that we want to do. We feel emptiness, disappointment, and distress. We feel that we stand against ourselves, against the purpose of our life. We feel uncomfortable. Through this distress we may immediately or eventually discover a better way of living and relating to life as a whole. The Inner Voice of God within us is the Distresser. It is a signal of warning in our computer every time we do something wrong.

Q&A

Question: *We read that enthusiasm is the Divine Fire. Is this one of the Names of God?*

Answer: As we said previously, God is Fire. We are told also that He is Electric Fire or Cosmic Fire, Solar Fire, and Fire by Friction or Chemical Fire. Those who contact Him become fiery, enthusiastic, inspired, and charged with fire.

Enthusiasm is a fire that you can use to drive your life — creating beauty and service, cultivating the consciousness of people, and organizing great fields of labor. But the highest use of the fire of enthusiasm is for a fiery involvement with the Path leading you to your divine destination.

A truly enthusiastic person with fiery aspiration searches for wisdom, searches for a Teacher, searches for co-workers, servers, books. He continuously educates himself, disciplines himself, prepares himself for a great service.

He does not wait for others to encourage and help him. He does it all by himself if people are not around him. He does not depend on others to progress on the Path and to render him service. He continues an enthusiastic life of service and spiritual discipline even if no one praises him or helps him.

He has the fire in him, and the fire propels him forward.

He does not depend on people and conditions. Enthusiasm creates the best conditions, and it draws those to him who will not be burdens on his shoulders.

If he sees a weakening of his fire, he knows how to feed it. He takes his fire from his Soul, from the Hierarchy, from his Teacher, from the books of wisdom, from his sacrificial service, from the joy of his heart, from the spring of the Common Good. There are so many places to take fire and make the fire of his enthusiasm bigger. He gets the fuel for his fire every time he sees unrighteousness, ignorance, hatred, and wars. His enthusiasm increases a hundredfold when he sees the sufferings and pain of the world because he knows that unless he travels on the path of perfection, he cannot be used for humanity.

An enthusiastic person is devoted to his meditation, to his Evening Review, to his studies, to his duties and responsibilities. He radiates fire because his inner being becomes radioactive.

You can compare two teachers who speak about the Teaching. One puts all his fire, heart, and spirit in it as he prepares it, as he delivers it. You sense in each of his sentences the fire of his soul which touches your soul. You see the future in his talks. You see Infinity, beauty, and sacrifice. The other one imparts information or emotions, and you feel you are facing a street that is a dead end.

I remember our Teacher gave a duty to one of our classmates. He said, "You are going to arrange the building of fourteen little huts as retreats for those who want to seclude themselves in meditation." You should have seen the fire in the Teacher's eyes. Our classmate was immediately charged with the fire of enthusiasm. He collected the right students around himself and, working day and night, the huts were finished in four months. All this time we never heard a complaint, never saw any anger or irritation. He was in complete joy.

Once I asked why he was so joyful. My Teacher said, "Do you not realize he sees already the completion of the work in my eyes?"

When all was finished, the Teacher spoke about him and concluded that he was an example of enthusiasm and dealt with the fire very intelligently.

Profiter

Profiter. All Names of God orient us toward unity. In this name we discover that He is like an Owner of a company, the benefit of which finally goes to Him. The benefit of each worker goes to His account. Anyone in the world who expands his consciousness achieves a high level of beingness and renders a sacrificial service to humanity. All is done for the profit of the *One*. All revenue flows to the same account. Since all people are part of God, the Whole God benefits from the achievement of each. He is the Common Treasury of experiences, knowledge, light, love, power, and beauty. We are His senses in the process of development. No one owns anything. Eventually all that is reality remains for Him. He inherits all that we become.

Light

Light. We had a Sufi master who used to say that every atom, every form, every living being, every globe, planet, sun, and suns have Him as their Light. It is He that is the Light in all manifestation. It is He that will illuminate and enlighten all pilgrims on the path toward Him.

He is the Light in all thinkers, creators, artists. He is the Light in Mothers, Fathers, in children. He is the Light in Leaders, in Teachers. We benefit from that Light according to our purity and spirit of striving. He is the Light of the stars. He is the Light of fireflies. He is the Light of seeds. He is the Light of all humanity. He is the Source of all Light.

The Guide

94

The Guide. He is the true Path in all paths. He is the Guide on all paths, in all human endeavors. He guides all travelers to their own central core, and each core becomes a door leading to the Core of All. He guides all living forms, inspiring them to their final destination, duties, and responsibilities on the Path.

Every kingdom, every living form receives its light from Him. He is the One Who warns us when we enter into the world of our hallucinations. If a person intelligently reviews his life, he will see how and in what moment the guidance came to him and how he either appreciated and obeyed the guidance or neglected it.

He guides on all levels and on all planes our thoughts, relationships, labor, and service if we have eyes to see his activities within us, within humanity, within all that exists.

Incomparable 95

Incomparable. First of all, no one can compare Him with anything because nothing exists besides Him. You cannot compare anything with something if that something does not exist. But even if you take Him as existing beside all that exists, you cannot find anything to compare to Him.

If you take a king, a genius, a wealthy man and compare them to Him, you realize that they are mere sparks in relation to His Cosmic Suns. If you try to compare His beauty with the manifested beauty of flowers, you prove to yourself the degree of your ignorance. In His Beauty, in His Power, in His Light, every worldly beauty, every kind of power, and every kind of light turn into nothing.

Everlasting

96

Everlasting. All existence, in all its parts, comes and goes. Some parts last a few billion years or more, but they slowly fade away and new existences take their place. Nothing lasts . . . except Him.

If we try to think about how many stars and Galaxies, how many worlds He manifested, and how many billions and billions of years the chains of manifestation have continued and disappeared and new creations have begun, our intellect enters into complete darkness. No one can understand the mystery of existence, the appearance and disappearance of all existence. Only *He remains* as the Cause of the whole phenomenon of space.

Inheritor

Inheritor. He inherits all that a spark of light, a human being, a planet, a sun, a Galaxy leaves behind after its disappearance. He inherits even our assets and debts. Wise ones think about what to leave behind — wealth or debts? Some existences on any plane try not to leave things that will bind them and urge them to come back and clean their mess. Some existences try to leave Light, Love, and Beauty to inspire them in their future journeys. What do we leave for God after we depart? This is a serious question.

The Path

The Path. There is no other path than Him. All true paths are strings in His Path. One day I imagined that every existence on every plane is a station on His Path. The Path is the power which leads the light in an atom to the Light existing beyond all existence. He waits for us on the Path at each station and leads us to the next.

Every living form on every plane is a path because He is the Path in them. He is the beginning of every path. His Path has no end. It is not true that He is the beginning and the end. He is only Endlessness, and because of this He has no beginning.

How can the human mind think without a beginning and without an end? But a human being can make a considerable breakthrough if he can for one minute start thinking without the concept of beginning and end. All is continuous. The Path does not start and does not end.

God is the only Path. All human life must walk on that Path.

Forbearer

Forbearer. A forbearing one not only is a person who has developed patience and forgiveness, but also he is one who knows how not to let his emotions, interests, expectations, and power interfere.

We are told that He does not hurry. He does not act under forceful and demanding conditions. He does not react but patiently waits and takes action only if that action will benefit the person and all that is related to the person. In forbearance we see also a strand of tolerance during which He observes how the person is acting, where he is directed, and under what influences he is working.

The forbearing one does not count days and years to take action. He knows that "Time is nought" and things can be corrected any time or guidance can be given any time. Forbearing evokes a soul response from the lives existing in any form, and this response makes these lives enter into the plans and purpose of the forbearer.

Forbearance is an electromagnetic energy leading people to their right destination. The Forbearing

One and the subject develop conscious contact with each other and create the opportunity to unfold.

 Allah — God

Allah — God, I am that I am, Tat Tvam Asi. What is there left to say?

In some Eastern texts they talk about one hundred and eight names instead of one hundred. And they use one hundred and eight beads. This is because they say the same name in many different ways: Krishna Gee, Krishna . . . .

Every Great One is a flowering of Him. He is flowering through them. For example, God is flowering through Jesus, Christ, Krishna, and so on. That is very beautiful. No matter how much they increase in number, it is better. The number 108 is a significant number because when you add 8 and 1, they become 9. This is the super achievement on the path of Infinity.

These are the names of God, but also they are words of power or mantrams. If you repeat them consciously and meditate upon them, you will make a great breakthrough into the mystery of your divine Self. There is Infinity within these words, and as you go deeper into them you transform all your beingness and change the way you are living.

One day while I was chanting one of the names of God, my Teacher advised me. He said, "It is a great and grave responsibility to chant His names or to meditate on His names because you are enter-into a zone of fiery energies. Be careful that mentally, emotionally, and physically you are pure so as not to be damaged by the fiery Source of energy which is *the One.*"

Second, he said, "I advise you to dedicate yourself to writing, playing music, dancing sacred dances, and above all working hard in manual labor so that excess energies accumulated within you are expressed and used creatively. You must charge your wires according to their capacity if you want to preserve your sanity and health. Remember, He is Consuming Fire."

Watch the children, the teenagers, the youth in the world. It seems that the majority have lost their path, and they do not think about God. He is something that does not exist or something that is not worth thinking of, since they have movies, television, radios, crimes, games, dates, fun. They have no time in life to think about God.

A young man asked me, "What benefit can I have thinking about His names?" I answered, "For one year be occupied with His names. Then we will talk."

Of course all these names are the reflections of the Sun on the broken glass of the mind of man. The Sun of suns stands beyond all definitions and characteristics, but each name can turn to us as a witness of the existence of the *Sun* if we use it to strive toward Him.

Each name of God opens a new window within our consciousness to look at Infinity, hear the call of Infinity, and respond to Infinity through striving toward perfection. Each day of our life we must try to transcend ourselves and feel His Presence every minute of our life.

Bibliographic References

Agni Yoga Society. New York: Agni Yoga Society.
Leaves of Morya's Garden, Vol. I., 1953.

Saraydarian, Torkom. Cave Creek, AZ: T.S.G. Publishing Foundation, Inc.
The Subconscious Mind and the Chalice, 1993.

Saraydarian, Torkom. Sedona, AZ: Aquarian Educational Group
The Bhagavad Gita, 1974.
Video — Why Drugs Are Dangerous, September 6, 1992.

The Great Invocation

From the point of Light within the Mind of God
Let light stream forth into the minds of men.
Let Light descend on Earth.

From the point of Love within the Heart of God
Let love stream forth into the hearts of men.
May Christ return to Earth.

From the centre where the Will of God is known
Let purpose guide the little wills of men —
The purpose which the Masters know and serve.

From the centre which we call the race of men
Let the Plan of Love and Light work out
And may it seal the door where evil dwells.

Let Light and Love and Power restore the Plan on Earth.

Index

A

Abaser — Humiliator, the, 48
Able One, the, 161, 163
Absolute, the, 159
Acceptance
 defined, 217
Accountant, the, 131
Accounting
 and God, 131
Advanced striving
 and balance, 174
Akbar, the Great, 72
All Merciful One, the, 17
All-Embracing One, 95
All-Self, 42, 170
Allah, 244
Angels
 as God, 197
Associative integration, 177
Atoms
 and Divine Mind, 184
Attacks
 and names of God, 144
AUM
 as name of God, 14, 144
Aura
 cleansing of, 143
Avenger
 three ways of, 219
Avenger, the, 219
Aware, One Who is, 63
Awareness, 63

B

Balance
 how achieved, 226
Balance and equilibrium, 173
Balance, need for, 191
Balancing device, 175
Balancing One, the, 226
Beauty
 as God, 83
Beauty, path of, 25
Beauty, Source of, 116
Beauty, the, 62
Behavior, mental, etc.
 and God consciousness, 177
Best Bestower, the, 35
Bestower of Wealth, 229
Bhagavad Gita
 people approach, 183, 187, 195
Bird, wings of, 171
Black holes, 161
Blessings
 and slander, 109
Bodies
 as lives, 204
Bodies in light
 and God consciousness, 175
Bodies, healthy
 reasons why, 173
Bodies, three
 dissolution of, 181
Bridge building
 between two poles, 171, 198, 217
Broom of God, 140

Buddha, 34, 151, 205
Buddhist temple
   and bowing to students, 78

C

Calamities
   and restrain by God, 230
Calculator, the, 84
Car, defects of
   and spiritual journey, 54
Cattle, being like, 164
Cause of existence, 202
Causes and existence, 93
Certainty and balance
   how created, 177
Chains of mind
   integration of, 178
Chinese and God
   as Space, 82
Christ, 14, 19, 40, 52, 91, 100, 107, 109, 112, 115, 122, 126, 133-134, 161, 188, 202, 205, 220, 245
   and seeing God, 14
Circuits of mind
   how to clear, 189
Civilization and culture
   and God, 117
Collector, the, 227
Compassion
   defined, 15
Compeller, the, 28
Conqueror, the, 34
Conquerors, future, 34
Conscious living
   and names of God, 45
Consciousness
   and result of elevation, 140
   two sides of, 171
Consciousness thread, 146
Consciousness, change of
   and meditation on God, 57
Consciousness, expansion of
   and betterment of life, 183
Consciousness, focus of
   and troubles, 175
Consolation
   defined, 222
Consoling One, the, 222
Constructor, the, 31
Contamination
   sources of, 143
Control, loss of, 69
Cosmic Symphony, 141
Creative power, 30
Creator, the, 10, 30

D

Death
   dealing with, 182
Deception, 91
Deeper One, the, 202
Deepest within
   and finding Father, 202
Departure
   and what is left behind, 240
Destroyer
   defined, 139
Destroyer, the, 139
Devoted One, the, 213

Devotion of God, 213
Diamond
    as example of God, 141
Dignified, the, 29
Dignity
    defined, 29
Disciples, real
    and success, 173
Dishonorer, the, 53
Diskettes of mind, 177
Distresser, the, 231
Divine
    how to be, 228
Dominant One, the, 165
Dominating ourselves, 166
Drug use, 186

E

Earthquake
    and commentary on God, 120
    and power of man, 165
Ego and vanity
    and excess of matter, 187
Emotions
    and strength, 121
Enthusiasm
    defined, 232
Ever-Living, the, 145-146
Everlasting, the, 239
Exalted
    defined, 50
Exalter, the, 50
Exhalted One, the Most, 211
Existence
    and Truth, 107
Existence with God, 169
Expands, One Who, 46

Expansion
    and names of God, 46
Experience
    as formulation, 201
Experience of Presence, 203
Eye of God, 91-92
Eye, big
    in temple, 57

F

Failure
    dealing with, 77
    how to view, 68
Failure and gain, 97
Faithful, the, 23
Fashioner, the, 32
Father and I are One
    explained, 202
Feeder, the, 74
Feeling, capacity of
    and names, 83
Fiery aspiration
    and increase of fire, 233
Fire
    as purifier, 221
Firm One, the, 122
Firmness, 122
First One, the, 169
Flowerings of God
    and Great Ones, 245
Focus of thought
    results of, 190
Forbearer, the, 242
Forests, trimming of, 185
Forgiveness, 68
Forgiver, the, 68
Free in nature
    and God's generosity, 88

Freedom, absolute, 224

G

Generous One, the, 87
Generousity
   defined, 88
Gifts of God, 35
Glorious One, the, 152
Glory
   and humiliation, 49
   defined, 152
Glory, Lord of, 225
God
   and being dead, 26
   and getting closer to, 32
   and result of being active, 118
   and what is provided, 135
   as a cause, 115
   as a Source, 116
   as cause of life, 116
   as Common Treasury, 235
   as dwelling in man, 81
   as guide, 237
   as mathematician, 84
   as nameless, 12, 82
   as new, 77
   as One Who never leaves, 125
   as the cause, 115-116, 147
   as transcendental, 41
   as witness, 105
   how to root in us, 10
   how understood, 11
   in primitive understanding, 9
   ways to understand, 10
God as action, 33
God as fire, 232
God consciousness, 171, 173-177, 179, 187-188
God, as the Ear, 199
God, being a part of, 112
God, being empty of
   and resulting problems, 117
God, creation of, 195
God, inner
   how to deal with, 185
God, knowing
   and self transformation, 14
God, names of
   108 or more, 245
   and creating locations in us, 212
   and levels of understanding, 200
   and progression in evolution, 193
   and responsibilities of chanting, 245
   and steps of integration, 179
   and dimensions of teaching, 199
   and times of crises, 166
   and why to have, 82
   as mantrams, 83
   as radiations, 43
   as seed thoughts, 196
   effects of, 81
   how to use, 190
   right or wrong, 198
   Tao, 13
   why to find, 193

why to study, 43-44
God, thinking about, 115
God, will of
    explained, 39-41
Gophers, living as, 153
Govern
    defined, 207-209
Governor, the, 207
Governors within, 209
Gracious One, the, 101
Gratitude
    and closeness to God, 128
    defined, 70
Great Architect, 84
Great Sage, the, 133
Greatness, seed of, 72
Guardian, the, 24
Guide, the, 237
Guilt
    how to deal with, 217

H

Hologramic unit
    as Universe, 105
Holy
    defined, 20
Holy One, the, 20
Honor, Lord of, 225
Humiliation, 48
Humility, 188

I

Ideas as energies, 146
Imagination
    as a source of attack, 143
Inclusiveness, 95
Incomparable, the, 238
Independent One, the, 228
Inheritor, the, 235, 240
Integrity
    built on, 42
Internal layers of bodies, 203
Internal One, the, 202, 205

J

Judge, the, 59

K

Karma
    and judgment, 59
Karma, creation of
    and explosive rings, 191
Karma, operation of, 40
Karmic Lords, 131-132
King, the, 19
Knower, the, 38
Knowing, all, 56
Knowingness, 129

L

Last One, the, 181
Law of Compassion, 15
Law of Incarnation, 40
Law of Karma, 15, 40
Law of the One Self, 42
Light of the World, 205
Light, the, 236
Limitations
    how to break, 46
    why to break, 103
Limitlessness, 47

Love as attractor, 221
Loving
    God and others, 92
Loving One, the, 99
Loving others
    for the One, 158

M

Magnificent, the, 67
Mahat
    defined, 185
Majestic, the, 85
Majesty
    defined, 85-86
Majesty, the Lord of, 225
Manifested One, the, 184
Masterpiece
    of human creation, 161
Matter
    being lost in, 174
Matter and Divinity
    balance of, 171
Matter side
    and Spirit, 176
Meditation, 33, 44, 47, 54, 82, 104, 144, 159-160, 183, 189-190, 192, 196, 200, 219, 233-234
Mental confusion
    and God consciousness, 177
Mental sickness, 178
Mercy
    of God, 17
Mightiness of God, 27
Mighty One, the, 26
Mind contents
    explosive sections, 189

Mind of God, 185
Morality, highest, 42
Moses
    and Will of God, 41
Mother's devotion, 213
Motionless One, the, 33

N

Names
    as energy, 83
Names of God
    as bridges of response, 194
    as given by various cultures, 8
    AUM, 14
    See also God
Names, layers of, 103
Nature
    as names of God, 193
    organization of, 31
Nature as God
    our attitude toward, 184
Nobility
    defined, 150
Noble One, the, 150

O

One Self
    and God, 41
One, the, 42, 63, 113, 157
Originator, the, 133, 135

P

Pain and suffering

and lack of devotion, 215
Path, 44, 53, 60, 115, 214, 219, 232, 237, 241
   and enthusiasm, 232
Path, the, 241
Patience
   development of, 168
Patient One, the, 65
Payment in life, 87
Peace, the, 21
Possibilities, 162, 205-206
Posthypnotic suggestions, 45
Postponer, the, 168
Power, Source of, 116
Power, the, 224
Praise
   need for, 78
Praiseworthy One, the, 128
Praising God, 128
Prayers
   how answered, 94
Preserve
   defined, 73
Preserver, the, 73
Process of understanding and meditation, 200
Profiter, 235
Progress
   as breaking limitations, 51
Protecting Friend, the, 125
Provider, the, 135
Psychiatry
   job of, 174
Punishment
   esoteric meaning of, 219
Purification
   and sounding names, 142

Q

Quickener
   defined, 137
Quickener, the, 137

R

Redeemer, the, 75
Religions
   and principles of, 91
Renunciation, self, 52
Repeating names, 141
Repentance
   and progress on path, 219
   three meanings of, 216
Repentance, the Acceptor of, 216
Responsive One, the, 93
Restrainer, the, 230
Resurrecting One, the, 103-104
Resurrection
   defined, 103
Revelation
   as result of meditation, 201
Revelations of God
   and constant change, 167
Revengeful God, 68
Right human relations, 96
Righteousness
   defined, 61
Righteousness, the, 61, 133
River flowing
   and human progress, 167

Roses
   in higher planes, 133

S

Saint Augustine
   and God, 9
Saint Francis, 63, 121
Saint Francis monastery, 121
Saint Paul, 10
Sanjaya
   and clairvoyance, 187
Screws, bucket of, 178
Sealing the door
   defined, 39
Seeing in layers, 204
Seeing One, All, 57
Self-Existing One, the, 147, 166
Self-praise
   and T.S. response, 151
Senses, to come to
   defined, 56, 60, 76, 199
Separatism, 95
Shamballa prayer, 162
Shoes and clothes
   as witnesses, 46
Sinner
   effect of being called one, 60
Slander
   and your value, 109
Soul, 56, 66, 138, 171, 217-219, 233
Spirit
   and matter, 176
Spiritual life
   seeing as is, 53

Spiritual nature
   how cultivated, 180
Standards
   creation of, 86
Story:
   of Armenian genocide / Will of God, 41
   of athletic games / being first, 169
   of beating girlfriend / elevating consciousness, 139
   of boxer / strength, 120
   of boy and dead friend / will of God explained, 40
   of boy and new girlfriends / firmness, 124
   of boys and birds / God consciousness, 176
   of Buddha's enemy / fighting against enlightenment, 34
   of burned house / detachment, 182
   of chanting names / need for purity, 245
   of children and ocean / mystery of creation, 129
   of couple and hitchhiker, 96
   of doctor and God / self-deception, 12
   of doctor and healing / limitness of knowledge, 129
   of drug seller / asking God, 118

of fourteen huts / fiery Teacher, 234
of girl and meditation / breaking habits, 104
of hungry man / response of God, 93
of King Akbar and enemies / becoming great, 110
of lady and prayer / God in all, 198
of man and names / meditation on 100 names, 58
of rich man and two sons / Father as friend, 126
of spacy man / need for balance, 172
of stolen wallet / God as trustee, 110
of T.S. and boys in mountains / the feeling of glory, 152
of T.S. and computer genius / the real creator, 186
of T.S. and father / being in space, 30
of T.S. and losing family / mental integration, 178
of T.S. and who is God / namelessness of God, 211
of T.S. visiting asylum / guilt complexes, 17
of T.S. writing books / seeing possibility, 163
of T.S., Teacher & violet flowers / Ever-Living, 145
of Teacher visiting monastery / feeling humiliation, 48
of three goats / patience, 65
of traveling Teacher / exalting others, 50
of two boys and blocks / limited understanding, 10
of wife and cheating husband / God as friend, 125
T.S. not liking himself / God as friend, 126
Strengthener, the, 52
Strong One, the, 120
Strong, becoming, 52
Stupidity
　vs. Able One, 164
Subconscious urges, 45, 207
Sublime, the, 71
Success
　two sides of, 173
Sufi Teachers
　and meditating on God, 44
Sugar and sweetness, 201
Sun's rays
　explaining names of God, 43
Sustainer, the, 36
Synthesis
　and balance, 226

T

Tactica Adversa, 98
Teacher, fiery
    qualities of, 233
Teenager car, 186
Television and radio
    and mental development, 120, 187
The Firm One, 122
The Great Invocation, 39
Thinking, integrated, 178
Thought, pure
    ascending, 133
Time concept, 148
Tolerant One, the, 221
Transformation
    process of going interior, 205
True Self, 24
Trustee
    defined, 109
Trustee, the, 109

U

Unemployment
    as a shame, 162
Unique One, the, 155
Unique, being
    defined, 155
Unity
    and balance, 226
Upanishads, 13, 68, 113, 158

V

Vibration of names, 142

Virtues
    as names of God, 87
Vision
    and strength, 121

W

Watchful One, the, 90, 112
Watchful, being
    defined, 90
Watching vs. witness, 112
Wealth, real, 229
Wisdom
    defined, 97
Wise One, the, 97
Witness, the, 105, 112
Women
    as balancers, 191
Words spoken
    and travel in Space, 46
Worshiping
    the One, 158

Z

Zorba, 182

About the Author

This is Torkom Saraydarian's latest published book. The author's books have been used all over the world as sources of guidance and inspiration to live a life based on the teachings of the Ageless Wisdom. Some of the books have been translated into other languages, including Armenian, German, Dutch, Danish, Portuguese, French, Spanish, Italian, Greek, Yugoslavian, and Swedish. He holds lectures and seminars in the United States as well as in other parts of the world.

Torkom Saraydarian's entire life has been a zealous effort to help people live healthy, joyous, and successful lives. He has spread this message of love and true vision tirelessly throughout his life.

From early boyhood the author learned firsthand from teachers of the Ageless Wisdom. He has studied widely in world religions and philosophies. He is in addition an accomplished pianist, violinist, and cellist and plays many other instruments as well. His books, lectures, seminars, and music are inspiring and offer a true insight into the beauty of the Ageless Wisdom.

Other Books by Torkom Saraydarian

The Ageless Wisdom
The Bhagavad Gita
Breakthrough to Higher Psychism
Buddha Sutra — A Dialogue with the Glorious One
Challenge For Discipleship
Christ, The Avatar of Sacrificial Love
A Commentary on Psychic Energy
Cosmic Shocks
Cosmos in Man
Dialogue with Christ
Dynamics of Success
Flame of Beauty, Culture, Love, Joy
The Flame of the Heart
Hiawatha and the Great Peace
The Hidden Glory of the Inner Man
I Was
Joy and Healing
Leadership Vol.I
Legend of Shamballa
The Mysteries of Willpower
New Dimensions in Healing
Olympus World Report...The Year 3000
Other Worlds
The Psyche and Psychism
The Psychology of Cooperation and Group
    Consciousness
The Purpose of Life
The Science of Becoming Oneself
The Science of Meditation
The Sense of Responsibility in Society
Thought and the Glory of Thinking
Sex, Family, and the Woman in Society

The Solar Angel
Spiritual Regeneration
The Subconscious Mind and the Chalice
Symphony of the Zodiac
Talks on Agni
Triangles of Fire
Unusual Court
Woman, Torch of the Future
The Year 2000 & After

Booklets

A Daily Discipline of Worship
Building Family Unity
Earthquakes and Disasters — What the Ageless Wisdom Tells Us
Fiery Carriage and Drugs
Five Great Mantrams of the New Age
Hierarchy and the Plan
Irritation — The Destructive Fire
Nachiketas
The Psychology of Cooperation
Questioning Traveler and Karma
Responsibility
The Responsibility of Fathers
The Responsibility of Mothers
Spring of Prosperity
Success
Synthesis
Torchbearers
What to Look for in the Heart of Your Partner

Videos

The Seven Rays Interpreted
Lecture Videos by Author

Ordering Information

Write to the publisher for additional information regarding:

— Free catalog of author's books and music tapes

— Lecture tapes and videos — complete list available

— Placement on mailing list

— New releases

— A free copy of our newsletter *Outreach*

Additional copies of *One Hundred Names of God*

U.S. $13.95 (Softcover)

Postage within U.S.A. $4.00
Plus applicable state sales tax

T.S.G. Publishing Foundation, Inc.
P.O. Box 7068
Cave Creek, AZ 85331
United States of America

TEL: (602) 502-1909
FAX: (602) 502-0713

T.S.G. Publishing Foundation, Inc. is a non-profit, tax-exempt organization.

Our purpose is to be a pathway for self-transformation. We offer books, audio and video tapes, classes and seminars, and home study courses based on the core values and higher principles of the Ageless Wisdom.

These fine books have been published by the generous donations of the students of the Ageless Wisdom.

Your tax deductible contributions will help us continue publishing and growing.

Our gratitude to all.